WELCOME

Chatsworth was built to welcome guests and to be seen. Over five centuries, members of my family have welcomed guests from around the world, and the house has been open for people to see round since the mid 1600s.

Sixteen generations of my family have lived here, and as you will discover each generation has made its own changes at Chatsworth. Some I find inspiring, some bewildering, but all of them intriguing.

My wife and I share a passion for collecting contemporary art and sculpture, and the contrast between the modern forms and materials, and this space steeped in history is one we enjoy. Many things fascinate us about Chatsworth, from the landscape with its seasonal changes, the 6th Duke's Emperor Fountain, and the great variety of historic textiles, but most of all, the people. Chatsworth would be nothing without people, the visitors and staff, who bring the place to life.

Every visitor has a different view, and there's always something new and extraordinary to discover. We hope you will enjoy discovering your own favourite things.

Stoker Devonshire   *Amanda Devonshire.*

The Duke and Duchess of Devonshire

CONTENTS

In 1552 Sir William and Bess began to build an ambitious new house, around a central courtyard with a gate tower, great hall and Chapel; however, little evidence survives today of Elizabethan Chatsworth. Its West Front was recorded in a needlework panel, and there is a painting of the house, copied from a lost original, which shows how it looked in the mid-17th century. The Hunting Tower was built in the 1580s and still stands on the hill behind the house. Another Elizabethan structure, known traditionally as Queen Mary's Bower, was used as a fishing platform and stands near the riverbank by the present bridge.

Bess married four times but only had children with her second husband, Sir William. Their second son, also William (1552-1625), became his mother's heir and bought Chatsworth from his older brother Henry. William was made Baron Cavendish in 1605 and created Earl of Devonshire in 1618. After her husband died in 1557, Bess married Sir William St. Loe (d.1565) and lastly, in 1567, George Talbot, 6th Earl of Shrewsbury (c.1528-1590). Queen Elizabeth I appointed Shrewsbury custodian of Mary, Queen of Scots, who was a prisoner at Chatsworth at

various times between 1569 and 1584. Her lodgings were on the east side of the house where the rooms, though since completely rebuilt, are still called the Queen of Scots Apartment. Bess also built Hardwick Hall, near Chesterfield, her surviving masterpiece. It belonged to the Cavendish family until 1957, when it was accepted by the Treasury in-lieu of death duty and given to the National Trust.

The estate of Chatsworth was acquired by the Cavendish family in 1549. Sir William Cavendish (1505-1557), one of Henry VIII's commissioners during the Reformation, and his young wife Elizabeth (c.1527-1608), also known as Bess of Hardwick, sold estates given to him by the Crown and bought land in Derbyshire close to Bess's childhood home. The estate was previously owned by the Leche family, and it is likely that there was a small manor house on or close to the site of the present house.

Top left: English School; *Bess of Hardwick as a young woman*, c.1550s

Top right: John Bettes the Elder; *Sir William Cavendish*, c.1552

Above: Photograph of Hardwick Hall, c.1900

Left: Attributed to Bess of Hardwick; *Needlework of Elizabethan Chatsworth*

Few alterations were made at Chatsworth until the late 17th century. In 1686 the 4th Earl of Devonshire (1640-1707) rebuilt the South Front, adding new family rooms on the first floor and a magnificent State Apartment, intended for the reception of a royal visit from William and Mary, the new King and Queen, on the second floor. In 1694 he was created 1st Duke of Devonshire for his part in bringing William III and Mary II to the English throne. The Duke originally intended only to alter the South Front, but he enjoyed building so much that once he started he could not stop. The East Front followed, including the Painted Hall and a long gallery, now the Library. George London and Henry Wise designed a formal garden on a grand scale. A Frenchman, 'Grillet', designed the Cascade, and Thomas Archer (1668-1743) designed the temple at the top. The artist Leonard Knyff (1650-1722) was commissioned to record the changes, but hardly had this been completed when the desire to build again proved irresistible.

The Duke went on to rebuild the West Front, and finally the North Front. In 1702 the Canal Pond was dug where there had once been a hill. William Talman (1650-1720) was the architect for the South and East Fronts. The West Front was perhaps designed by the Duke himself, working closely with his master builder, and the North, with its bow front, by Thomas Archer. The new Chatsworth was finished just before the Duke died in 1707.

The 2nd Duke (1673-1729) made no changes to the house and garden he had watched being created in his youth. He made his mark in a different field, as a collector of paintings, drawings and prints. He also made important collections of coins and carved Greek and Roman gems. This Duke was the grandfather of Henry Cavendish (1731-1810), the distinguished and eccentric scientist, who determined the composition of water, recognised hydrogen as an element, and was 'the first man to weigh the world'. Cavendish's collection of 12,000 books on science and many other subjects is today in the Library at Chatsworth.

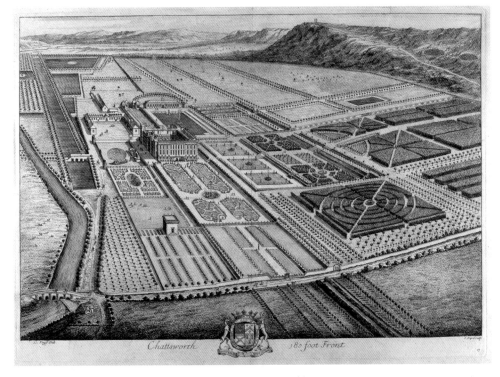

Above: Charles Jervas; *Portrait of William Cavendish, 2nd Duke of Devonshire*, 1710s

Left: Johannes Kip after Leonard Knyff; *Engraving of Chatsworth*, 1699

The 3rd Duke (1698-1755) served for seven years as Lord Lieutenant of Ireland and was a Member of Parliament from 1721 until he moved to the House of Lords following his father's death in 1729. When Devonshire House in Piccadilly, London was burnt down in 1733, the 3rd Duke commissioned William Kent (c.1685-1748) to rebuild and furnish it. Much of Kent's furniture for Devonshire House, which was sold in 1919 and subsequently demolished, is now at Chatsworth.

Like his father, the 4th Duke (1720-1764) was a prominent Whig politician and served as Lord Lieutenant of Ireland and Prime Minister of England (November 1756 - May 1757). He made great changes to the park and garden which had been begun by his father. He decided that the house should be approached from the west, and demolished the 1st Duke's stables and offices which interfered with the view on this side.

He also relocated the nearby village of Edensor, building new housing for his staff and tenants further away from the house.

Top: B. Green; *Devonshire House*, 19th century

Above: William Marlow; *A view of Chatsworth*, c.1770

The architect James Paine (c.1716-1789) was commissioned to build new stables up the slope to the north-east, and these were completed in 1763. In 1762 the course of the river was altered and Paine designed a new bridge upstream of the house. Land to the west of the river, including what remained of Edensor village, was enclosed to become the park as it is today. Lancelot 'Capability' Brown (1716-1783) was engaged to naturalise the appearance of the park and formal baroque garden, although some of this work probably began the generation before under the guidance of William Kent. The 4th Duke married Lady Charlotte Boyle (1731-1754), the only surviving daughter and heiress of the architect and connoisseur Richard Boyle, 3rd Earl of Burlington (1694-1753). This marriage brought new estates to the Cavendish family, including Lismore Castle in Ireland, Londesborough Hall and Bolton Abbey in Yorkshire, and Burlington House and Chiswick House in London. The inheritance included all of Lord Burlington's architectural books and drawings, as well as the contents of his various houses including a wealth of Old Master paintings and important furniture, decorative arts and antiquities.

Right: George Knapton; *Portrait of Lady Charlotte Boyle, Baroness Clifford and Marchioness of Hartington,* 1748-1756

Bottom left: Thomas Hudson; *William Cavendish, 4th Duke of Devonshire,* mid 18th century

Bottom right: *Lismore Castle and the river Blackwater*

The 5th Duke (1748-1811) married Lady Georgiana Spencer (1757-1806), daughter of the 1st Earl Spencer, who became a celebrated socialite and leader of fashion. She and her great friend Lady Elizabeth Foster (1757-1824) were painted several times by Sir Joshua Reynolds (1723-1792) and Thomas Gainsborough (1727-1788). Although Lady Elizabeth subsequently became the mistress of the Duke and had two children by him, this did not interfere with her friendship with Georgiana. The *ménage à trois* in which they lived continued for some years. After Georgiana's early death in 1806, the 5th Duke married Lady Elizabeth. Georgiana and the Duke had three children together. The eldest, also Georgiana, married the 6th Earl of Carlisle. Her daughter Lady Blanche Howard married her cousin William Cavendish, who eventually became the 7th Duke.

The Duke and Georgiana lived mainly in London, but when they did come to Chatsworth they filled it with friends and relations, writers and politicians. The house was open for visitors to look around, and on one day a month dinner was provided for whoever visited. John Carr of York (1723-1807) was commissioned by the Duke to redesign the decoration and furnishings of the private apartments in the neoclassical taste.

Above: Sir Edwin Henry Landseer; *Portrait of William Spencer Cavendish, 6th Duke of Devonshire, 1831-1832*

Left: Thomas Gainsborough; *Portrait of Georgiana, Duchess of Devonshire, 1785-1787*

The 6th Duke (1790-1858) succeeded his father in 1811 at the age of 21. He is remembered as the 'Bachelor Duke' because he never married. He loved entertaining his friends and spent 47 years improving his many houses and collecting objects of every kind with which to embellish them. He bought two complete libraries, having inherited his mother's love of books, but his principal collecting passion was for sculpture. He engaged the architect Sir Jeffry Wyatville (1766-1840) to build the North Wing at Chatsworth, including a purpose-designed gallery for his sculpture collection. Lismore Castle in County Waterford was also later substantially rebuilt. Such expenditure taxed even the 6th Duke's resources and he was forced to sell property in Yorkshire, including most of the town of Wetherby and his estate at Londesborough.

The Duke became intensely interested in gardening after he met Joseph Paxton (1803-1865), a young gardener working in the Horticultural Society's gardens at Chiswick which adjoined the Duke's own garden there. He appointed Paxton to be head gardener at Chatsworth in 1826 and together they changed the garden, creating much of what is seen today. Plant-collecting expeditions were sent to the Americas and

India, giant rockeries were built, and the 'Conservative Wall' glasshouse was built. In 1844 Paxton designed and constructed the Emperor Fountain, the jet in the Canal Pond which reached over 85 metres (280 feet) on a calm day.

It was an engineering feat which entailed draining the moor into an eight acre man-made reservoir on the high ground above the house. The whole of this ambitious scheme was completed in six months. The most famous of Paxton's achievements at Chatsworth was the building of the Great Conservatory, constructed in wood, iron and glass, (destroyed in the 1920s).

William Cavendish (1808-1891), 2nd Earl of Burlington of the second creation, became the 7th Duke in 1858. He was grandson of the 6th Duke's uncle Lord George Cavendish. He married Lady Blanche Howard (1812-1840), the 6th Duke's niece. Blanche died aged 29, and was mourned by her husband and her uncle for the rest of their lives. Chatsworth was a very quiet place during the thirty years of the 7th Duke's tenure, and he decreed strict economies after the extravagance of his predecessor. He is best remembered today as the developer of Eastbourne in East Sussex and Barrow-in-Furness in Cumbria.

Left: Photograph of Sir Joseph Paxton, 1850s

Above: Charles Baugniet; Engraving of the 6th Duke and his family, 1852

The 8th Duke (1833-1908) was a statesman who served in Parliament for over fifty years. A towering figure in the Liberal Party, he played a leading role in the cabinets of Gladstone and later Liberal governments. Three times he was asked by Queen Victoria to become Prime Minister, but each time he refused. In 1886 he split the Liberal Party over his opposition to Home Rule for Ireland. In 1892, at the age of 59, the Duke married Louise von Alten (1832-1911), widow of the Duke of Manchester. He and the 'Double' Duchess, as she is sometimes known, entertained lavishly at Chatsworth, usually during the autumn and winter. King Edward VII and Queen Alexandra were regular visitors to these house parties.

The 8th Duke and Louise had no children, so when he died in 1908 he was succeeded by his nephew Victor Cavendish (1868-1938). The 9th Duke and his wife Lady Evelyn Fitzmaurice (1870-1960), daughter of the 5th Marquess of Lansdowne (Viceroy of India 1888-1894), had seven children. He was a Member of Parliament from 1891, and like all of his predecessors loved politics and continued to attend the House of Lords after the death of his uncle. He held office as Financial Secretary to the Treasury and from 1916 to 1921 was Governor-General of Canada. When the Duke and Duchess moved to Chatsworth in 1908 a lot of work had to be done to the house, including the complete renewal of the drainage system. Duchess Evelyn became very knowledgeable about the contents of the various houses, while her husband was an attentive landlord and enjoyed his farming and sporting activities.

Left: Sir John Everett Millais; *Portrait of Spencer Compton Cavendish, Marquess of Hartington, later 8th Duke of Devonshire*, 1887

The 9th Duke was the first to have to pay death duties, which amounted to over £500,000 (£53 million today). Added to the even greater running debt left by the failure of the 7th Duke's business ventures, this forced some major sales. All the Caxton books in the Library and the John Kemble collection of plays, including many rare first editions of Shakespeare, were sold in 1912 to the Huntington Library in California. Devonshire House and its three acres of land in Piccadilly, London was sold in 1919.

Bottom left: Edward Hughes; *Portrait of Louise, Duchess of Devonshire, 1896*

Top right: Philip Alexius Laszlo de Lombos; *Portrait of Victor Cavendish, 9th Duke of Devonshire (1868-1938) in the robes of the Chancellor of Leeds University, 1924*

Bottom right: John Singer Sargent; *Portrait of Evelyn, Duchess of Devonshire (1870-1960) when Lady Evelyn Cavendish, 1902*

When Edward Cavendish (1895-1950) succeeded his father as 10th Duke in 1938 he and his wife, Lady Mary Cecil (1895-1988), daughter of the 4th Marquess of Salisbury, planned to make many alterations and improvements at Chatsworth. However, a year later saw the outbreak of World War II and Chatsworth became home to the girls and staff of Penrhos College.

In May 1944 the Duke's eldest son William, Marquess of Hartington (1917-1944) married Kathleen Kennedy (1920-1948), sister of President John F. Kennedy. Four months later he was killed in action in Belgium while serving with his regiment, the Coldstream Guards. Kathleen died in an aeroplane accident in 1948. They had no children, so the Duke's second son Andrew Cavendish (1920-2004) became his father's heir and succeeded to the title in 1950.

The 10th Duke's death at the age of 55 was sudden and unexpected, and death duties at 80% had to be paid. Nine of the most important works of art and many rare books, as well as Hardwick Hall and its supporting farms and woods, were surrendered to the Treasury in lieu of cash. Thousands of acres of land and other assets were also sold. The negotiations took 17 years to complete and the final payment was made in 1967.

At this time the 11th Duke and his family lived at Edensor House on the other side of the park. In 1959 they moved back to Chatsworth after some internal modernisation was done, including the installation of a new central heating system. A new kitchen was fitted closer to the family's dining room and six flats were made for members of staff and their families.

The 11th Duke married the Hon. Deborah Mitford (1920-2014), daughter of Lord Redesdale, in 1941. He served in the Coldstream Guards during the war; on 7 December 1944, he was awarded the Military Cross in recognition of gallant and distinguished services. The action took place on 27 July 1944 when his company was cut off for 36 hours in heavy combat near Strada, Italy. After the war he was Mayor of Buxton from 1952 to 1953. He was also a minister in the Conservative government 1960-1964. The Duke and Duchess had three children, Emma (b.1943), Peregrine [Stoker] (b.1944) and Sophia (b.1957).

Lady Emma married the Hon. Toby Tennant in 1963 and they have three children. Lady Sophia has two children and is married to Will Topley. Stoker married Amanda

Heywood-Lonsdale (b.1944) in 1967 and they have three children, William, Earl of Burlington (b.1969), Celina (b.1971) and Jasmine (b.1973).

By November 2000, the 11th Duke had held the title for 50 years and he remains the longest serving head of the family. During his time as Duke, he and Duchess Deborah worked tirelessly to ensure the survival of Chatsworth after the enormous price of the 1950 death duties. They established the successful visitor attraction which Chatsworth has become, and under their management the retail shops, catering outlets, Estate Farm Shop and the farmyard and adventure playground were all added. As well as all these new businesses, following the outbreak of foot and mouth in 2001 Christmas opening was introduced as a way of extending the season that year. It has since become one of the most successful and busy times of year.

In addition to their entrepreneurial skill, the 11th Duke and Duchess Deborah instigated many new features in the garden and brought about a renaissance in terms of collecting contemporary art, a family passion and activity which had essentially laid dormant since the 6th Duke's death in 1858.

On his death in May 2004 he was succeeded by his son Stoker. The 12th Duke and Duchess moved into Chatsworth in January 2006. In 2007, following a thorough assessment of the fabric of the building and its services, a programme of repairs, maintenance and restoration was started to preserve Chatsworth for the long-term future.

Opposite: Photograph of the wedding of William Cavendish, Marquess of Hartington and Kathleen Kennedy, May 1944

Right: Group photograph on the occasion of Lady Sophia's christening, 1957 with 11th Duke and Duchess, Lady Emma and Marquess of Hartington

Through the Chatsworth House Trust, the registered charity which operates the house, garden, park and the farmyard and adventure playground, a £14 million restoration project known as the 'Masterplan' began in 2008. This project has enabled visitors to experience the house, garden and estate as never seen before.

Contemporary art has always been at the heart of Chatsworth, from the 1st Duke's Baroque interiors and decorative arts, to the new sculpture acquired by the 6th Duke in the 19th century, to the renaissance in collecting which began with the 11th Duke and Duchess and continues under the present Duke and his Duchess today. There is also an ambitious programme of temporary loan exhibitions of modern and contemporary art, including the annual

Sotheby's selling exhibition *Beyond Limits* which takes place in the garden every autumn. Throughout the year there is a series of special events, including the *Chatsworth International Horse Trials* in May, the *Chatsworth Country Fair* in September, and *Christmas at Chatsworth*.

Above: 12th Duke and Duchess of Devonshire

Opposite: Lord and Lady Burlington with their children, James, Elinor and Maud

HOUSE PLAN

The Tour
Ground Floor

1. North Entrance Hall
2. North Sub-Corridor
3. Painted Hall
4. Inner Court
5. Grotto
6. Chapel Corridor
7. Oak Room
8. Chapel

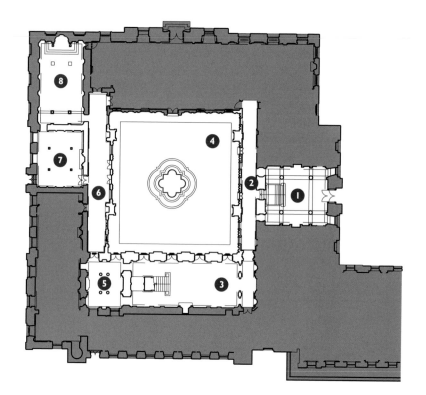

Second Floor

9. Great Stairs
10. Great Chamber
11. State Drawing Room
12. State Music Room
13. State Bedchamber
14. State Closet
15. Old Master Drawings Cabinet
16. South Sketch Gallery
17. West Sketch Gallery
18. North Sketch Gallery Lobby
19. North Sketch Gallery
20. Guest Bedrooms
21. Alcove Room

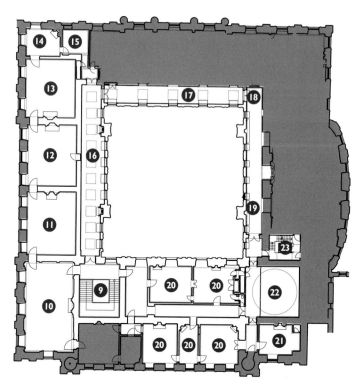

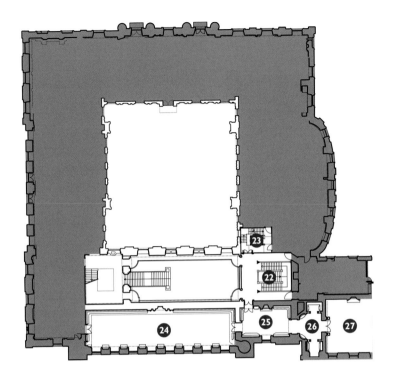

First Floor

22. Oak Stairs
23. Back Stairs
24. Library
25. Ante Library
26. Dome Room

North Wing

27. Great Dining Room
28. Vestibule
29. New Gallery
30. Sculpture Gallery
31. Orangery Shop

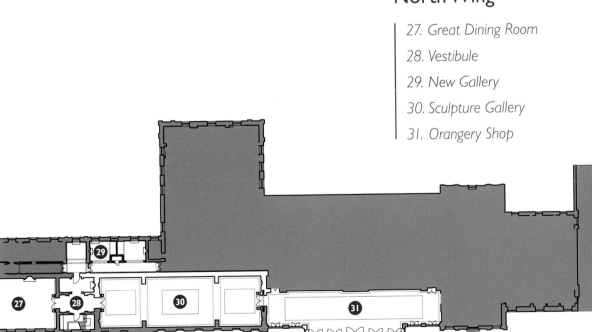

"The open wood fire makes this otherwise rather gloomy space into what it should be - a welcome to the house for all our visitors."

12th Duke of Devonshire

From 1760 onwards this room has served as the principal entrance for visitors to the house, the original entrance being through the doors at the centre of the West Front. The hall was created for the 4th Duke by James Paine (1717-1789) who remodelled the original kitchen here. That room was double the height of the present Hall, and occupied the same position in the building as the Elizabethan kitchen. At the same time as this room was converted, the 4th Duke radically changed the approach to Chatsworth, moving the bridge up stream to the north to create the picturesque drive through the valley to enhance the views of the house. The fireplaces and the staircase were subsequently altered for the 6th Duke by Jeffry Wyatt (1766-1840) in 1823-1824. The staircase is constructed of Derbyshire limestone, full of crinoid fossils, and known locally as 'once-a-week marble'. This stone features throughout the house.

The four columns around the centre of the room are copies of one in the gardens at Chiswick on the outskirts of London. That house, built by the 4th Duke's father-in-law the 3rd Earl of Burlington (1694-1753), formed part of the important inheritance which doubled the size of the Devonshire estates and art collection.

The two large sculptures are Roman, 1st century AD. They were discovered at Apt in France, and were acquired by the 6th Duke, a passionate collector of sculpture, at the Wanstead House sale in 1822. The large painting above one of the fireplaces was commissioned by the 6th Duke from Sir Edwin Landseer (1802-1873). It depicts a romanticised view of Bolton Abbey imagined as it might have been before the dissolution of the monasteries. The figure of the kneeling man presenting a stag to the Abbot was posed for by the 6th Duke's Russian coachman.

Above: Sir Edwin Henry Landseer; *Scene in the olden time at Bolton Abbey*, c.1834

Left: Roman; A Statuary Group of a Lady and her Daughter, c.100 AD

"On coming into this passage, you are struck with the exceeding beauty of the pavement"

6th Duke of Devonshire

"Alas!, we cannot agree with the 6th Duke that even his elaborate pavement takes the eye off the dreadful little door into the quadrangle, or that any observant visitor could fail to notice the wretched architecture of the new corridors on three sides of the house."

Duchess Evelyn

Originally an open colonnade to the central courtyard beyond, this space was enclosed in the 1820s for the 6th Duke to create a more convenient corridor. The elaborate geometric pavement, composed of different coloured marbles, was made by an Italian craftsman called Leonardi, who lived in the Forum at Rome. The 6th Duke recalled that when first laid in 1841 due to "…the brightness of its polish, it was difficult to make anybody tread upon it." The intention of the pavement was to distract the eye from the fact that none of the doors or windows are symmetrically aligned on the courtyard or the North Entrance Hall.

Around the walls are sets of mahogany chairs and benches, designed as hall furniture by William Kent (1685-1748). The chairs were made in the 1720s for Chiswick and the benches in the 1730s for Devonshire House in London. The brackets supporting sculpture and candelabra appear to be carved stone, but are actually cast iron. The paintings are predominately 17th century, and many were in the collection of the 3rd Earl of Burlington at Chiswick.

Above: William Kent; Hall Bench Settee 1733-1740

Right: William Henry Hunt; *The Gallery, Chiswick House*, 1822

"The annual Christmas party for schoolchildren is held in the Painted Hall and is as noisy and cheerful as can be. The highlight of the evening is the arrival of Father Christmas."

Duchess Deborah

Occupying the same location as the Elizabethan Great Hall built for Bess of Hardwick and Sir William Cavendish in the 1550s, the Painted Hall is the largest and grandest room in the original house. It has undergone three major changes in its history, the most striking element being the reconstruction of the staircase rising to the first floor, which has been rebuilt twice.

Dominating the room is the painted decoration which gives rise to its name, the only part of the interior which survives from its creation in 1687-1694. The paintings were painted by Louis Laguerre (1663-1721) and depict scenes from the life of the Roman General Julius Caesar (100-44 BC). The long east wall shows him offering sacrifice at the Temple, flanked by oval scenes, painted in imitation of carved stone, which illustrate his journeys across the Rubicon river (left) and the English Channel (right). The 1st Duke deliberately chose the subject of

Caesar for the decoration in an attempt to flatter the new protestant monarch, William III (1650-1702). A group of seven English aristocrats, including William Cavendish, then 4th Earl of Devonshire, had invited William III to take the throne with his wife Mary II in 1688. In 1694 William and Mary rewarded the 4th Earl for his support by making him 1st Duke of Devonshire.

Perhaps as a reminder to William not to exceed his legitimate power, the scene on the north wall above the entrance to the room shows the assassination of Caesar by the members of the Senate. Between the windows the walls are painted with large arrangements of arms and armour in the style of Roman trophies, and the openings at the top of the staircase, recall the architectural form of a Roman triumphal arch, complementing the Roman theme of the interior.

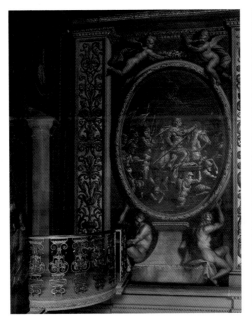 

Above left: Louis Laguerre; *Caesar crossing the Rubicon*, 1689-1691

Above right: Louis Laguerre; *The assassination of Julius Caesar*, 1689-1691

The present staircase, and the catwalk gallery below the windows, were created in 1912 for the 9th Duke and Duchess Evelyn. The balustrades are copies of the 17th-century balustrade on the Great Stairs above, and were made by the Arts and Crafts Workshop of the Bromsgrove Guild. The 1912 staircase replaced one built for the 6th Duke in the 1820s to designs by Jeffry Wyatt. Duchess Evelyn commented that it "…had a balustrade that would have been a disgrace to any London area. "The 6th Duke himself noted that the former staircase, built in 1691 with two curved flights enriched with carved alabaster, marble and the local quartz mineral Blue John, was "much handsomer".

In 1936 the ceiling was discovered to be sagging and on the point of collapse. Over the course of two years the floor above was reinforced and the original plaster reattached before all the cracks were filled and the painting restored. In 1996 the ceiling was cleaned and conserved again, and the walls in 2005-2006.

Top: The Painted Hall, c.1890

Above: The inscription over the fireplace: "These beloved ancestral halls begun in the year of English liberty, 1688, were inherited by William Duke of Devonshire in 1811, and completed in the year of his sorrow, 1840"

Opposite: William Henry Hunt; *The First Duke's Staircase in the Painted Hall,* 1827

"Since we cleaned the Inner Court and gilded the windows on the east side in 2010, this is a much brighter and more cheerful place."

Duchess of Devonshire

The stonework of the Inner Court was cleaned and conserved in 2008-2009. The project, part of the Masterplan restoration of Chatsworth begun in 2007, took 60 weeks to complete. During that time the courtyard was filled with a forest of scaffolding poles, all of which had to be taken out via the Painted Hall.

One of the principal achievements of the project was the conservation of the four remaining carved stone trophies that decorate the east façade, carved by Samuel Watson (1662-1715), Chatsworth's master carver. Before the creation of corridors around three sides of the court in the 1820s, the space was larger, and more richly decorated. Originally there were twelve trophies (on the same scale as the surviving four), and life-size sculptures standing in niches where the French doors into the Painted Hall are now. In addition there were two further sculptures flanking the door in the centre of the west façade, and open colonnades formed of paired columns painted pea green on the south and north sides. The colonnades supported a gallery

topped with carved stone busts, some of which now stand on top of the 1st Duke's Greenhouse in the garden. The courtyard was designed to impress everyone who entered the house at a time when they crossed the courtyard on their way to the Painted Hall.

The stone used to build Chatsworth was quarried some two miles from the house. The same stone is being used to conserve the house today. The masons who undertook the replacement of lost carving from the trophies inserted discreet modern carvings underneath the armour skirts on the two outermost trophies. Symbols of modern-day warfare - a peace poppy, rifle and a tank, all carved in low-relief, now form part of these 17th-century expressions of military power.

The windows on the east façade, the only ones to survive from the 17th century, are gilded with 24ct gold-leaf. Evidence for the original gilding of windows and some carved decoration on the building survives in the 1st Duke's Accounts.

Below left: Detail of the restored stone carving showing the modern tank and poppy

Below right: Armorial trophies carved by Samuel Watson, c.1689

"The fountain was brought to life again in 1999 when the stone flags were taken up and the pipes reconnected so that water now flows from the leaden tongues of the dolphins."

Duchess Deborah

The Grotto, an entirely stone space which supports the Great Stairs above, is enriched with applied carvings in Roche Abbey stone. On the ceiling is the Garter Star, the insignia of the Order of the Garter, an honour presented to each Duke from the 1st to the 11th. These, together with the carved garlands of fruit and flowers and the sea creatures framing the relief of the Goddess Diana, were all carved by Samuel Watson.

Chatsworth has contained contemporary art throughout its history. The bas-relief of Diana at her bath above the fountain was new when it was acquired by the 1st Duke in London in 1692. Today contemporary art still features, continuing the tradition of patronage and collecting by the family.

Displayed in the window is *Tablepiece XCIV*, 1969 by Sir Anthony Caro (1924-2013). It was acquired by the Duchess' mother, Mrs Heywood-Lonsdale. In the centre of the room stands *Sheaf of Light* by Tim Harrison (b.1952), which was acquired in 2000.

Hanging on the wall opposite the fountain is a contemporary portrait of Laura, Countess of Burlington, the 12th Duke and Duchess's daughter-in-law. A digital portrait by the artist Michael Craig-Martin (b.1941), it represents the sitter with a simple line drawing, and the colour fills of each area are constantly changing. The computer determines the selection of colours, as well as their intensity and brightness, on an ever-changing cycle. The combinations are random and endless, and the portrait will never look the same twice.

Top left: Bas-relief of Diana at her Bath, 1689

Top right: Michael Craig-Martin; *Digital Portrait of the Countess of Burlington*, 2010

Above: Detail of the Garter star on the Grotto ceiling carved by Samuel Watson, 1689

"In 2011 we gathered together all the Gardom tables which were scattered throughout the house and used them to display a variety of minerals and smaller antiquities."

12th Duke of Devonshire

Like the North Sub-Corridor (before the Painted Hall), this corridor was enclosed by the 6th Duke in the 1820s. He also had the central bay added to increase the width, and brought the fireplaces, designed by James Paine in the 1760s, from the North Entrance Hall. The combined result was a far more comfortable and convenient access to the Chapel.

In 2010 the corridor was redisplayed to evoke a grand collectors' gallery, bringing together representative examples of the Devonshire Collection spanning over 4,000 years of human creation. Old Master paintings, including works by Jacopo Tintoretto (1519 - 1594), Salvator Rosa (1615-1673) and Pietro da Cortona (1596-1669) are displayed alongside ancient Egyptian, Greek and Roman sculpture. The fragment of a colossal foot from a giant Acrolithic statue of a goddess dates to the 1st century before Christ and the two Egyptian granite statues of Sekhmet, from

the temple of Mut at Karnak were carved in the 18th Dynasty (1386-1349 BC). In addition the impressive mineral specimens (collected by the 11th Duke in the late 20th century), are gathered together underneath a set of 17th-century tables with ironwork by a local blacksmith, John Gardom (1664-1713) who worked alongside the French craftsmen Jean Tijou (late 17th-early 18th century).

Displayed in and around each of the fireplaces is a site specific commission by ceramicist Edmund de Waal (b.1964). They echo the arrangements of 17th-century ceramics in the State Apartment on the 2nd floor. Inspired by a large show of de Waal's work in the Lake District in 2005, the 12th Duke and Duchess commissioned an installation from him. The eventual result, described by the artist as a 'cargo of pots' evokes the rhythm of music with the undulating heights of the various pots. Each pot is glazed in varying shades of white, and some feature tiny flashes of gilding.

Below left: Egyptian figure of the Goddess Sekhmet from the Temple at Karnac, 1386-1349 BC

Below right: Edmund de Waal; *Sounding Line*, detail, 2004

"One day, walking with a friend in Berner's Street, we were tempted into the auction-room, and found carved oak being knocked down…the fittings of some German monastery, and the woodwork of an old-fashioned pew… What discussions might be raised upon it hereafter! - what names given to the busts!"

6th Duke of Devonshire

The unusual oak panelling of this room, from which it now takes its name, was fitted between 1839 and 1841 for the 6th Duke. At that time it was referred to as the Summer Breakfast Room. It has had many different uses in its history, including being the storehouse for the library, manuscripts and records of experiments of the 4th Duke's cousin, one of the world's greatest scientists, Henry Cavendish (1731-1810).

Inset into some of the panels are small cupboards, the doors of which are concealed by small oil paintings. Ten of these record the 6th Duke's holidays, eight being of the north-east coast of England, painted by John Wilson Carmichael (1800-1868). Between the French doors and the window is a pair of paintings depicting some of the 6th Duke's favourite dogs. On the other wall, nearest the doors to the garden, is a more recent painting of two of the Duchess's dogs, FTCH Talsbrook Rhum of Bolton Abbey and FTCH Roberto Rannaldini of Bolton Abbey, by the artist Jemma Phipps (b.1977).

The model of Chatsworth, made in 1979, illustrates the various stages of building construction that created the house. The original square courtyard house built by the 1st Duke between 1687 and 1707 is at one end of the model. It stands on the footprint of its Elizabethan predecessor, and has the three ranges of corridors added to three sides of the courtyard in the 1820s. Running the rest of the length of the model is the North Wing, added by the 6th Duke to the designs of Jeffry Wyatt (1766-1840), in the 1830s. It demonstrates the impressive scale of the new building, and the three distinct entrances underneath the three arches.

Left: Carved heads of clergymen, detail of panelling

Top: John Wilson Carmichael; *Priors Haven, Tynemouth,* 1845

Bottom: Jemma Phipps; *Portrait of two of the Duchess of Devonshire's gundogs,* 2009

> *"This is the least changed room in the house and was inspired by the now lost Chapel at Windsor Castle."*
>
> 12th Duke of Devonshire

The Chapel was built between 1688 and 1693, a year before the 4th Earl was created 1st Duke of Devonshire. It has remained almost completely unaltered ever since. Occupying the same location as the Elizabethan Chapel, this double-height space stands directly beneath the State Bedchamber and Closet above.

The altarpiece, constructed of alabaster quarried at Castlehayes near Tutbury in Staffordshire, and black marble from Sheldon moor above Ashford-in-the-Water some five miles away, is a tour-de-force of architecture and interior decoration by Chatsworth master carver Samuel Watson (1662-1715). Only the two standing figures of Justice and Prudence are by another hand, the Danish sculptor Claus Gabriel Cibber (1630-1700), who was responsible for carving the majority of the garden statuary. Watson was also responsible for the carved pendants which enrich the cedar panelling. His drawings for these pendants, and many other carved details at Chatsworth, survive in the archives, as do the payments for many of the fittings of the 1st Duke's house such as the £360 paid in London for the pair of large gilt-brass candlesticks that stand on the steps of the altarpiece.

The focal point of the altarpiece is the oil painting of *The Incredulity of St. Thomas* by Antonio Verrio (1639-1707). The painted decoration on the walls and ceiling is by Louis Laguerre and his assistant Ricard, both of whom had previously worked as Verrio's assistants. The Royal Chapel at Windsor Castle, painted by Verrio a few years earlier, served as the inspiration for the Chapel at Chatsworth. The principal scene on the wall opposite the windows presents Christ Healing the Sick, which is believed to be a reference to the restoration of the nation's religious health by the removal of

a Catholic King (James II) from the throne. The 1st Duke employed a Chaplain, and the household staff would have attended daily prayers, sitting in the body of the Chapel whilst the family would have been in the gallery above.

Top left: Samuel Watson; *Alternative design for the altarpiece in the Chapel*, late 17th century

Bottom left: Samuel Watson; Detail of the head of a Cherubim, late 17th century

Top right: Caius Gabriel Cibber; Figure of Faith from the altarpiece, 1688-1691

"When we moved to Chatsworth in 2006 we decided that this site worked best for Carefree Man who welcomes every visitor with the doffing of his hat."

12th Duke of Devonshire

Left: Caius Gabriel Cibber; figure of Apollo, 1688 and bust of Mark Antony, English late 17th century

Centre: Great Stairs

Below: Samuel Watson; Alabaster door case

Opposite: Italian, Bust of Apollo, late 17th century

Rising from the first to the second floor is one of the earliest examples of a cantilevered staircase in England, which attracted comment for the ingenuity of its construction almost as soon as it was completed in 1691. It provides a suitable herald for the grandeur in the State Apartment to which it leads. The complex decoration is evidence of the changing and developing taste of the 1st Duke - the walls are enriched with both painted and sculpted cycles of decoration. The steps have a gilded iron balustrade, made by the French Huguenot designer and blacksmith Jean Tijou (late 17th-early 18th century). He also worked at Hampton Court for William III and Mary II, and arrived at Chatsworth in 1688, being paid £250 for this balustrade.

The 1st Duke's original intention was to have walls painted with figures acting as a continuation of the ceiling painting by Antonio Verrio (1639-1707), which depicts the *Arrival of Cybele on her Chariot*, bringing plenty and abundance. As goddess of the Earth, Cybele was chosen to flatter Queen Mary, suggesting that through her reign Britain would prosper and flourish. An example of this can be seen on the far side of the ceiling, opposite the window, where a cornucopia overflows with gold coins, medals and other treasures. The coins are painted as if pouring over the cornice onto the upper part of the wall below. Today these coins, with the accompanying figures, appear ghost-like, unfinished or partly scrubbed out. This is

due to the later introduction of sculptures originally carved for the garden by Cibber, and busts that once stood in the Chapel which were brought here and added to the upper levels of the walls in 1692.

The lower levels of decoration are painted in imitation of sculpture, and show Bacchanalian processions. Bacchus, Roman god of wine, was often used to represent revelry and feasting, and his inclusion here is an allusion to the hospitality that visitors to Chatsworth should expect. The ceiling and wall paintings were all cleaned and conserved in 1997-1998.

> *"This great unappropriated apartment, which consumes in useless display the best habitable part of the house. What bedrooms might have been here with the south sun, and beautiful views! I was much tempted, but finished conservatively by repairing the sinking floors and threatening ceilings and, as a museum of old furniture and a walk in bad weather, I am well contented to retain this dismal, ponderous range of Hampton Court-like chambers."*
>
> 6th Duke of Devonshire

Apartments of state in secular houses were intended for the reception of the reigning monarch, and the resident family would not have lived in the rooms themselves. The layout and sequence of rooms is derived from the apartments in royal palaces in London and continental Europe. The decoration and furnishing of these interiors was lavish and of the highest quality to be found in the house. Occupying the position of the Elizabethan Long Gallery of Bess of Hardwick's house, they are unusually placed on the second floor of the building, not on the first floor as would be expected in the late 17th century. This compromise in planning is because initially the 1st Duke only intended to rebuild this south range of the house, and expected to preserve the rest of the Elizabethan building.

The rooms were made accessible to 'tourists' in the 17th and 18th centuries, including the celebrated authors and diarists Celia Fiennes (1662-1741), Daniel Defoe (c.1660-1731) and Horace Walpole (1717-1797), all of whom wrote and published their observations. By the 19th century the rooms had become deeply unfashionable, and their survival without major alteration is unusual. They were first used for their original purpose by a visiting monarch in 1913 when George V and Queen Mary stayed at Chatsworth, using the State Bedchamber as their bedroom.

In 1939 the rooms were emptied and used as dormitories for Penrhos College, a girls boarding school evacuated to Chatsworth during World War II. The atmosphere of

this time was captured by Edward Halliday (1902-1984) who recorded the State Drawing Room in a painting.

In 2006-2007 the State Apartment was redisplayed following an in-depth research project, in order to evoke a clearer sense of how they might have looked when first furnished.

Opposite:
Top right: Edward Irvine Halliday; *Chatsworth in Wartime: the State Drawing Room as a dormitory*, 1939

Bottom left: Fireplace in the Great Chamber decorated with Delft flower vases

Above:
Top: Detail of a Queen Anne coffer faced with panels of 17th-century Chinese Coromandel lacquer and English Bantam Work, 1705-1715

Bottom: Louis Laguerre; Detail of the ceiling in the State Bed Chamber, c.1690

Right: Looking east through the enfilade of the State Apartment

> *"Except as a lobby to Their Majesties' rooms during their visit this room has never been used. We cannot persuade our guests to mount so far up after dinner."*
>
> Duchess Evelyn

Completed in 1694, this was the principal room of the apartment where the Court would have assembled to await the King and Queen. It also served as a room for occasional dining, and the large buffet display of silver-gilt plate and oriental porcelain, garlanded with wax and silk flowers, has been set up to illustrate that use. The carved limewood which decorates the panelling contains representations of dead game, fish and fowl, another reference to the possible use of the room for eating. Of equal quality to the work of the more celebrated Grinling Gibbons (1648-1721), the carvings were often believed to be by that master until the discovery of Samuel Watson's name in the 1st Duke's Building Accounts. When new the carvings would have appeared very pale against the golden coloured oak, a distinction lost over time due to the oxidisation of the limewood and atmospheric pollution.

The ceiling, painted by Antonio Verrio (1639-1707), depicts the *Triumph of the Virtues over the Vices*. Figures representing virtue are presided over by the goddess of Justice, Astraea, who governed the Golden Age, a mythical time when mankind was in a state of innocence. The allegory here suggests she can now return because of the blessing of William and Mary's reign. Figures representing vice are driven down in the scene. Atropos (one of the three Fates) is shown cutting the thread of life with her 'abhorred sheers'. Verrio, who was quarrelsome with the 1st Duke's housekeeper, chose to paint this character as a portrait of the servant Mrs Hackett, thereby immortalising her on the ceiling.

Assembled in the fireplace is a group of flower vases and urns, a customary display during the summer months when a fire was not required. Each of the spouts on the vases would have held an individual bloom grown in the hothouses in the garden. The vases and urns were made in Delft from tin-glazed earthenware, a technique employed in Holland to imitate Oriental porcelain in the late 17th century. When first built, the views of the garden beyond the windows would have been an important feature of the room. At that time the layout was very formal, in the French style of gardening, with terraces and geometric plantings and with a large Parterre to the south before the Canal Pond. This was mainly swept away in the mid-18th century by William Kent (1685-1748) for the 3rd Duke, followed by Lancelot 'Capability' Brown (1716-1783) for the 4th Duke.

Below: Antonio Verrio; Detail of Mrs Hackett from the ceiling, c.1691

Centre: Display of Delft flower vases

Right: Samuel Watson; Detail of limewood carving

"The Coromandel furniture was at Hardwick when I first saw it, but belongs in this house because the pieces of seventeenth-century Chinese lacquer from which it is made lined the walls of the State Dressing Room, from 1692 to 1700, when they were removed."

Duchess Deborah

This room served as the first withdrawing room in the apartment, into which select members of the Court could retire from the Great Chamber. The ceiling, by Louis Laguerre, depicts an Assembly of the Gods. In the coving there are smaller scenes telling the story of the affair between Venus, goddess of love and Mars, god of war. Vulcan, Venus's husband who was responsible for forging weapons, is outraged when he discovers the infidelity.

The Mortlake Acts of the Apostle tapestries date to the mid 1630s, and were woven from designs by the Renaissance artist Raphael (1483-1520), originally made for tapestries which decorate the Sistine Chapel in the Vatican. Having been fixed in their present frames by the 6th Duke the tapestries had not been removed from the wall since the 1830s until 2014 when a major conservation project was begun. The large tapestry on the wall opposite the windows had deteriorated from exposure to light and atmospheric pollution. It was taken down and washed at a specialist facility and a lengthy programme of stitch repairs commenced.

The furniture is presented against the wall, as was the tradition in the 18th century, chairs only being brought into the centre when they were required. The cabinet opposite the windows and the two similar ones are made of Chinese lacquer, and take their name from the Coromandel coast from where they were exported to Europe. Crowded on top of the cabinets are displays of Chinese porcelain, highly prized in Europe when the secret for creating true porcelain had not yet been discovered in the West.

The pair of elaborately carved throne chairs were given to the 4th Duke as a perquisite (perk) for his role at the coronation of George III and Queen Charlotte in 1761. They are unusual in that they were carved by a woman, Catherine Naish (active 1759-1772). The lion and unicorn supporters from the Royal coat of arms sit on the cresting rails at the top of each throne flanking the ciphers of George and Charlotte. The seats and back are upholstered with an elaborate yellow silk, woven with floral sprigs and enriched with silver thread which has now tarnished to black. The silk was woven in the famous textile centre of Spitalfields to the east of the City of London.

Top right: Samuel Watson, Detail of carved limewood overdoor

Above: Catherine Naish, Coronation Chair of King George III, c.1771

> *"I first saw the French cuir repoussé at Fontainebleau: it suits the old Chateau perfectly, and it does well here, but there is too much gilding and colour employed on it in this room."*
>
> 6th Duke of Devonshire

Top left: René Dubois; Boulle marquetry cabinet supporting a portrait bust of Louis XIV (1643-1715), King of France

Top right: Jan Van der Vaardt; *Trompe l'oeil Violin and bow hanging on a door,* c.1723

Below: Marquetry panel from one of a pair of Louis XIV première-partie boulle marquetry and giltwood cabinet stands

Formerly called the Second Withdrawing Room or the Green Velvet Room, the changes made by the 6th Duke in the 1820s caused it to become known as the State Music Room. He inserted the central door on the wall opposite the windows to connect the space to the new gallery behind, improving the communication around the second floor. One of Chatsworth's most famous works of art, the *trompe l'oeil* painting of a violin hanging on a door was placed inside the new opening in 1836. Painted by Jan van der Vaardt (c.1653-1727), it survived the disastrous fire that destroyed old Devonshire House, the family's London residence in Piccadilly.

The stamped and gilded leather which covers the walls replaced the 18th-century green velvet which originally decorated the room. Different generations of the family have either liked or disliked the leather, and in the early 20th century Duchess Evelyn covered it over with green fabric hangings. In the frieze at the top of the wall the 6th Duke had his portrait set in repeating roundels, something he later regretted, considering it to be too vain.

Today the room celebrates the 6th Duke's influence, bringing together much of the furniture by, or in the manner of André-Charles Boulle (1642-1732), the French cabinet maker who worked for Louis XIV, King of France. His distinctive technique of decorating the surface of furniture with veneers of pewter, brass and turtleshell with gilt bronze mounts enjoyed a revival in the 19th century when the 6th Duke was redecorating Chatsworth. Some of the pieces have been in the collection since they were made, others he purchased as antiques.

The majority of the paintings here were in the collection of the 3rd Earl of Burlington, and formed part of the inheritance of the 5th Duke. To the left of the violin door is the *Blind Belisarius Receiving Arms*, once believed to be by Van Dyck, but now attributed to Luciano Borzone (1590-1645). On the right of the door is the mythological subject of *Acis and Galatea* by Luca Giordano (1634-1705).

"We restored the bed to its former height and had the fabric of the bed, copied to make new curtains. At the same time we hung tapestries over the 6th Duke's leather: one room of this is quite enough."

Duchess of Devonshire

The 1st Duke spent more on furnishing this room than any other in the house. The mirror which hangs between the windows was particularly expensive, mirror glass being very difficult to make in such large sheets. Unusually it is signed by its maker, John Gumley (active 1694-1729), and dated May 1703.

The ceiling painting, by Louis Laguerre (1663-1721), depicts the goddess Aurora (dawn) chasing away the goddess Diana (night), making an appropriate subject for a bedroom. Today the walls are hung with 17th-century Brussels tapestries, also of mythological subjects, returned as part of the rearrangement in 2006-2007. They are hung loosely over the stamped and gilded leather added by the 6th Duke.

The present bed was made for Kensington Palace, and is the bed in which George II died. It was claimed as a perk by the 4th Duke for his position as Lord Chamberlain and brought to Chatsworth. In 2006-2007 an extensive conservation project on the

bed was undertaken, revealing that it had been lowered by 47cm at some point in its history. The original height has been reinstated and once more the decorative feet, formed as fluted columns, can be seen. The 1764 inventory of Chatsworth revealed that within the State Apartment only this room, and the Closet next door, had curtains. New pull-up curtains were made for the windows in 2006, using a crimson silk damask that is a reweave of the textile on the bed.

The silver-gilt toilet service on the dressing table is the most complete example of Parisian silver from this time. Used during the morning ritual *levée* when a lady would dress and prepare herself for the day, it was made by Ferry Prévost (active late 17th century). Each piece is decorated with the arms and monogram of William of Orange and Mary, (later William III and Mary II), and was probably given by Mary to the then Countess of Devonshire in recognition of her husband's support during the Glorious

Revolution. Standing on the floor to the right of the bed is a silver perfume burner. Another rare survival, it is used daily to burn incense to fragrance the room as was the practice in the late 17th century.

Top left: John Gumley Mirror, 1703, with a pair of Delft flower vases, c.1690 on a Queen Anne wrought-iron table, c.1700, flanked by a pair of Louis XIV boulle marquetry torchères, 17th century

Top right: Philip Rollos; Perfume Burner, c.1690

Above: Ferry Prévost, detail of the coat of arms of Mary II from a silver-gilt toilet service, 1694

"We had a fireplace made in imitation of one at Hampton Court - using spare fragments of carving to finish it. I collected some Blanc de Chine from various bedrooms to decorate the shelves."

Duchess Evelyn

Top left: Coffer faced with panels of 17th-century Chinese Coromandel lacquer

Top right: English Silver Chandelier, c.1694

Above: Detail of mantelpiece constructed in 1912

The State Closet was reconstructed as an oak panelled interior like all those which precede it only six years after its completion in 1694. Originally the walls were covered with colourful lacquer, now only present in the room in the form of the low cabinet to the left of the fireplace. In addition to the lacquer on the walls, mirrored piers decorated the corners of the room.

Today the walls display a range of oriental porcelain, as was fashionable in the late 17th century. Mary II had established this porcelain mania in England, creating rooms filled with these treasured ceramics. Above and below furniture, massed on mantelpieces, hung on the walls or standing on decorative brackets, no space was unfilled. The stepped chimneypiece was installed in 1912 for the 9th Duke and Duchess Evelyn and is an adaption of a design at Hampton Court Palace. Duchess Evelyn recalled that the 1st Duke's silver chandelier, which had been stored at Hardwick for many years, was brought to Chatsworth at the same time as the fireplace was created. Having searched for a suitable room to display it, she settled on the Closet stating that: *"A cloud is an insubstantial thing from which to hang such a heavy object, but it does not do to be hypercritical."*

"This Cabinet room was created in 2012 allowing us to show visitors a small but rotating selection of Old Master Drawings for the first time. The light levels are kept low to protect the very fragile works on paper."

12th Duke of Devonshire

Created in 2012 for the specific purpose of displaying in themed exhibitions some of the 3,000 Old Master Drawings collected by the 2nd and 3rd Dukes, this room evokes the feel of a collector's cabinet of the 18th century. Private spaces for the contemplation of highly prized works of art, natural curiosities or treasured items, cabinets first appeared in the 16th and 17th centuries.

In addition to the changing displays of drawings by celebrated artists such as Raphael (1483-1520), Leonardo da Vinci (1452-1519) or Sir Peter Paul Rubens

(1577-1640), the room contains a display of 17th-century ivories, Limoges enamel and a 16th-century dish by Bernard Pallisy (c.1510-c.1590). Behind the glass screen is a Roman pietra dura cabinet of the 17th century, its surface covered with mosaic panels in different hardstones. Above it is one of the greatest paintings in the collection, *Portrait of an Oriental* by Rembrandt van Rijn (1606-1669), believed to represent 'King Uzziah stricken with leprosy'. Signed by the artist and dated 1639, it was purchased in 1742 by the 3rd Duke.

Above: Detail of Roman pietra dura cabinet, 17th century

Right: Rembrandt van Rijn; *A man in oriental costume (possibly King Uzziah stricken by leprosy),* 1639

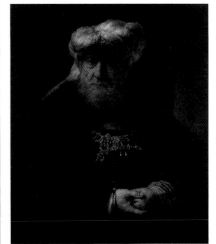

> *"In 2009 the Chatsworth textiles team made all the curtains and pelmets: in all there is over one kilometre of hand sewing."*
>
> Duchess of Devonshire

The Old Master Drawings collection is what gives this and the next gallery the name 'Sketch'. Fortunately - for the preservation of the drawings - they were rescued by Duchess Evelyn and returned to dark storage. The cabinet created for them in 2012 provides a more suitable display space than these galleries.

In 2009, following an 18 month project to reopen the windows to the courtyard and redecorate the space, the South Sketch Gallery became home to a display of the taste, collecting and patronage of the 5th Duke and Duchess Georgiana from the late 18th century. The portraits to the right of the central cabinet include the 5th Duke by Pompeo Batoni (1708-1787), painted on his Grand Tour of Italy. It is flanked by Duchess Georgiana on the right and her closest friend Lady Elizabeth Foster on the left, both painted by Sir Joshua Reynolds

(1723-1792). The 5th Duke, Duchess Georgiana and Lady Elizabeth Foster lived in a *ménage-à-trois* at Devonshire House. Following Georgiana's death in 1806 the Duke married Lady Elizabeth.

The furniture is all in the neoclassical style fashionable in the late 18th century. The giltwood chairs and sofas, part of larger suites, were made by Francois Hervé (active 1781-1796) for Chatsworth and Devonshire House. At the far end of the Gallery is a group of mahogany furniture made by the German cabinet maker David Roentgen (1743-1807). Based in Paris, he supplied royal and aristocratic clients with sophisticated mechanical furniture - the apparently simple dressing table here opens to reveal different elements.

Displayed in cabinets specially designed for them are mineral specimens collected by Georgiana. An unusual collecting activity for a woman at this time, it represents one of her many interests. She was also a bibliophile, patron of the visual arts and was declared by contemporaries as "...the Empress of fashion". The famous portrait of her by Thomas Gainsborough (1727-1788) is displayed in the centre of the group to the left of the main cabinet. Sold for 10,100 guineas in 1876 (the highest price ever paid for a painting by that date) it was subsequently stolen and taken to America. Eventually retrieved and resold, it was purchased for the Chatsworth House Trust in 1994.

Top: Pompeo Girolamo Batoni; *Portrait of William Cavendish, 5th Duke of Devonshire*, 1768

Top left: David Roentgen; Dressing table, 1785

Bottom left: Thomas Gainsborough; *Portrait of Georgiana, Duchess of Devonshire*, c.1785-1787

"…Richard, Earl of Burlington, our great grandfather, the architect of Chiswick and of the Colonnade at Burlington House."

6th Duke of Devonshire

This gallery displays works of art and objects associated with the great architect Earl, Richard Boyle, 3rd Earl of Burlington (1694-1753). Father of Charlotte Boyle, wife of the 4th Duke, all of his property and collections were ultimately inherited by the 5th Duke when he was 21 in 1769.

The 3rd Earl of Burlington championed the Palladian revival in this country and sought to transform taste in the early 18th century. His most influential work was the small villa he designed and built as an adjunct to Chiswick House in Middlesex in the 1720s. His portrait of 1743 by George Knapton (1698-1778) hangs to the right of the central window in the gallery. It shows him wearing the insignia of a Knight of the Order of the Garter, holding his publication on the English Renaissance architect Inigo Jones (1573-1652). Behind him is a bust of Jones, and the actual bust, a copy of the full-length statue of him at Chiswick by Michael Rysbrack (1684-1770) can be seen

on the pedestal to the right of the portrait. On the left is another bust, depicting his other architectural hero Andrea Palladio (1508-1580). Palladio was the Italian Renaissance architect who first correctly interpreted and revived the architecture of ancient Rome.

On the opposite wall are Old Master paintings arranged in the manner which Burlington hung them at Chiswick. The furniture below is all designed by Burlington's *protégé* William Kent (1685-1748). Kent travelled with Burlington on his Grand Tour and was first employed to paint ceilings at Burlington House in Piccadilly. He went on to design interiors for some of the greatest buildings in England including St James's Palace and Devonshire House in London and Houghton Hall and Holkham Hall in Norfolk. Kent's furniture designs were elaborate and sculptural, as shown by the examples in this gallery which come from Chiswick and Devonshire House.

Above: Benedetto Luti; *Portrait of William Kent,* 1718

Middle: William Kent; *Armchair,* c.1733-1740

Right: Busts of Andrea Palladio and Inigo Jones, flanking George Knapton's portrait of *Richard Boyle, 3rd Earl of Burlington,* 1743

> *"…probably unique as a record of a family by that compelling painter, a great friend who seemed to paint us."*
>
> Duchess Deborah

The largest painting, *Large Interior, London, W.9*, 1973 is a portrait of the artist's mother and his then girlfriend Jacquetta Eliot, painted in his London home. It was acquired in 1974. On the other wall is a group of portraits of the Cavendish family including: *Lady Anne Tree*, c.1950, *Portrait of a Woman, (Mary, Dowager Duchess of Devonshire)*, 1969, *Portrait of a Man, (Andrew Cavendish, 11th Duke of Devonshire)*, 1971-1972, *Woman in a White Shirt, (Deborah, Duchess of Devonshire)*, 1958-1960, and *Portrait of a Man (The Marquess of Hartington, now 12th Duke of Devonshire)*, c.1962.

Top: Lucian Freud; *Woman in a white shirt (Portrait of Deborah, Duchess of Devonshire)*, 1958-1960

Below left: Lucian Freud *Head of a woman (Portrait of Lady Anne Tree)*, c.1950

Below right: The Duchess of Devonshire and Lucian Freud in the artist's studio, 2004

Assembled here is a group of portraits by the 20th-century British painter Lucian Freud (1922-2011). The 11th Duke and Duchess Deborah were friends of Freud's since the 1950s, and commissioned and collected his paintings for over 50 years.

These five informal portraits of different members of the same family represent the lasting friendship that existed between them and the artist. This group exemplify the development in Freud's approach to portraiture and his handling of paint.

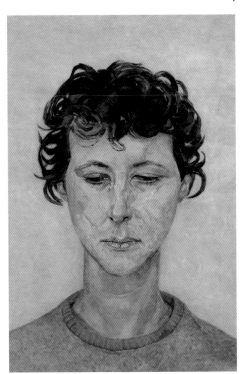

"In the Everyman portrait areas are highlighted by mirrors where the viewer or visitor becomes part of the portrait; in effect a self portrait of everyone. Highlighting the importance of visitors to Chatsworth, it is of significance that it is the central portrait, symbolic of our common humanity and of a more democratic age."

Jacob van der Beugel

Above: Jacob van der Beugel

Details of ceramic DNA panes from the North Sketch Sequence, 2014

The theme of family portraiture continues in this gallery. The space was formed in 2009 from a series of small bedrooms and service rooms in order to provide a continuous route around the second floor for visitors.

The installation on the walls of 659 ochre coloured, handmade ceramic panels is the work of Jacob van der Beugel (b.1977) and was realised in 2014. A pupil of Edmund de Waal (b.1964), van der Beugel was inspired to create a series of five abstract portraits using wall tiles when he was asked to create a ceramic space as a complement to the displays of historic ceramics in the cases. Following several discussions with the family and the Chatsworth House Trust he was commissioned to make the work in 2010. It forms the most significant single art installation at Chatsworth since the creation of the 6th Duke's Sculpture Gallery in 1832.

The portraits are based on the mitochondrial DNA of the 12th Duke and Duchess, their son Lord Burlington and his wife Lady Burlington. Their DNA was sampled via mouth swabs which were sent to a lab for sequencing. The four columns of blocks on each panel represent the four nitrogen containing bases which make up the characteristic double helix of DNA. Unique aspects of each individual's DNA sequence are captured on these blocks using variations in colour and surface treatment, while glazed blocks are arranged in response to a subject that is important to each individual. The 12th Duke chose his favourite walk around the garden at Chatsworth, and the Duchess chose her favourite piece of music, John Rutter's 'A Gaelic Blessing'. Lord Burlington asked to be shown surrounded by his family, while Lady Burlington chose a traditional stitching pattern she was taught as a child by her grandmother. This unusual and creative take on the traditional portrait creates a unifying scheme of decoration down the south wall of the gallery.

The fifth portrait, which is on the central pier, depicts Everyman, showing the DNA which we all have in common. Inserts of mirror in place of some of the blocks allows the viewer to see their own unique likeness reflected in the portrait. The north wall of the gallery is covered with ceramic framed mirrors which reflect the DNA panels and the light from the courtyard on the south side.

"The great want of lodging room here caused their alteration…there was nothing, therefore, to lament in their destruction and the gain is immense in accommodation."

6th Duke of Devonshire

Above: detail of an 1830 window pelmet in the Queen of Scots Dressing Room

Top left: Queen of Scots Dressing Room

Top right: Wellington Bedroom

The 6th Duke set about converting the rooms in this part of the house into new, convenient and fashionable bedrooms for his guests in 1830. Previously the rooms had been in a style like those in the State Apartment, but of a lesser quality and lacking painted ceilings. The apartments take their names from Mary Queen of Scots (1542-1587) who sometimes stayed at Chatsworth during her imprisonment, and Robert Dudley, Earl of Leicester (1532 or 1533-1588), favourite of Queen Elizabeth I (1533-1603) who visited as a guest of Bess of Hardwick and her fourth husband, the 6th Earl of Shrewsbury (1528-1590). It had long been believed that the rooms had been preserved from the Elizabethan house, although given the later structural alterations below this would have been impossible.

Today the rooms are presented as they might have been used in the late 19th century for the large house parties that were an integral part of country house life at Chatsworth. During the day guests would often go hunting or shooting, or tour the pleasure gardens. This was followed by large formal dinners with as many as nine courses, after which entertainments such as music, charades or amateur theatricals would take place. Ladies would often return to their bedroom up to six times a day to change their clothes for the different activities. Guests would usually bring their own ladies' maid or valet with them and they would need to be accommodated in the servants' rooms in the attics.

These suites of rooms are the most complete examples of bedrooms from this period to survive with their original furnishings. The hand-painted Chinese wallpaper and sugar-glazed chintz fabrics are typical of Regency and Victorian taste of the 19th century. The beds are richly carved and gilded and hung with elaborate draperies. The hangings are undergoing conservation by the Chatsworth Textile Department in order to preserve them for the future.

"This Staircase, connected with the Painted Hall above and below, was one of Sir Jeffry Wyatville's best efforts. He rather wished to add another flight of steps to the floor above, but that I resisted."

6th Duke of Devonshire

"The model for this extra flight is still at Chatsworth: we too resisted the idea of adding it though we did think hard about it first."

12th Duke of Devonshire

The 6th Duke and Wyatville removed the four floors that once divided this space in order to create this grand staircase. It connects the Baroque house with his new North Wing and its suite of grand reception rooms above a new range of domestic service apartments, built between 1818 and 1832. In 1928 the space was altered to reflect changes in taste, and in an attempt to more closely unite its style of decoration with the old house. In 2009 the space was restored to its original Wyatville scheme. The principle feature is the dome and lantern that tower above and provide light for the stairs.

The walls are hung with family and royal portraits ranging from the 1st Duke to the 11th Duke. On the large wall opposite the head of the stairs are different members of the family. The central portrait of a man on horseback shows the 1st Duke painted when he was 4th Earl in around 1670.

Below is a group portrait of the 3rd Earl of Burlington and his family with a servant. It is by Jean-Baptiste van Loo (1684-1745) and was painted in 1739, being delivered to Burlington House on Christmas Eve. Lady Burlington and her elder daughter Dorothy are both portrayed as artists.

On the wall to the right is a pair of portraits recording the coronation of Tsar Nicholas I of Russia (1796-1855) and his Tsarina. Painted by George Dawe (1781-1829) they were commissioned by the 6th Duke who was a close friend of the Tsar. Underneath the second floor gallery is the portrait of the Acheson sisters by John Singer Sargeant (1856-1925). These sisters were the granddaughters by her first marriage of Duchess Louise. The artist had wanted to paint the sisters using some of the poses they adopted when playing golf, but instead this more conventional representation of Edwardian elegance was chosen.

Left: George Dawe; *Portraits of Tsar Nicholas I of Russia and Empress Alexandra Feodorovna, consort of Tsar Nicholas I*, 1828-1831

Centre: John Singer Sargent; *Portrait of the Acheson Sisters*, 1902

"The books compose four libraries. One I found here, another in London, the third was Mr Henry Cavendish's and the fourth, Dampier, Bishop of Ely's."

6th Duke of Devonshire

"One of the 'libraries' to which the Sixth Duke refers is that of Henry Cavendish (1731-1810), the eminent scientist and great eccentric. His manuscripts and library of scientific and other books are still at Chatsworth, each stamped with 'H. Cavendish' on the back of the title-page."

Duchess Deborah

The 6th Duke inherited his mother's and his uncle's passion for books. He brought together the extant family collections and then set about increasing the size and quality of the library through various purchases.

In 1815 he converted the 1st Duke's Long Gallery, here, into a room to hold his ever growing collection. Within ten years he had commissioned Wyatville to remodel the space again and the present mahogany bookcases and the gallery running round three sides of the room are the result. The ceiling, with plasterwork by Edward Goudge (active late 17th century) and paintings by Antonio Verrio (1636-1707) are the only parts of the 1st Duke's interior to have survived. The enormous carpet, woven in three sections, is an Axminster and was designed to follow the painted roundels.

Today there are over 17,000 books in the Library and Ante Library covering six centuries. It includes the majority of the autograph writings of the 17th-century philosopher Thomas Hobbes (1588-1679), the scientific manuscripts of Henry Cavendish (1731-1810), the man who calculated how to weigh the Earth, and some of the architectural library of the 3rd Earl of Burlington. There are also medieval illuminated manuscripts and early printed books of the 15th and 16th century. In total the collection numbers some 40,000 volumes. Until the mid-20th century the Old Master Drawings were also stored here in portfolios before they were removed to a special environmentally controlled store.

The furniture in the Library comes from many different family houses. The four book tables, two at each end of the room, were designed by William Kent for the Library at Chiswick. The large suite of seat furniture attributed to Morrell and Hughes was brought from the Saloon at Devonshire House. In 2013 it was restored and reupholstered with a reweave of the original turquoise and gold silk brocade.

Left: Daniel Girard Elliot *Pavo Christitus* from *A monograph of the Paradiseidae, or Birds of Paradise,* New York, 1873

Centre: Attributed to Morell and Hughes; Detail of a settee

Right: John James Audubom; *Puffin* from *The Birds of America,* London, 1827-1838

Above: A gilt-bronze oil lamp mounted with antique Leopards head, c.1810

Opposite: Raffaele Monti; detail of the Veiled Vestal Virgin, 1846-1847

This small room forms the junction between the corner of the Baroque house and the 6th Duke's North Wing. The doors are off-set from the centre of the room to enable all the doors in the preceding and following rooms to align. Wyatville's screens of columns and bays to either side help to disguise this asymmetry along with the richly decorated white and gold ceiling.

In the centre of the room is a 19th-century bronze cast of the famous Renaissance statue of Mercury, messenger of the gods, by Giambologna (1529-1608). The marble doorcase is flanked by a pair of vases made of a very rare marble called *occhio di paone* or 'peacocks eye'. In the bay on the right is one of Chatsworth's most recognised works of art, the Veiled Vestal Virgin, 1847, by Raffaelle Monti (1818-1881). It featured in the 2005 film production of *Pride and Prejudice* with Kiera Knightley as Elizabeth Bennett and Matthew McFadden as Mr Darcy. The prop bust of Mr Darcy, made of wax, is displayed in the Orangery Shop.

In the bay on the left is a gilt-bronze oil lamp set with a leopard's head carved in onyx. The gilt bronze is 19th century, but the hardstone head is antique, believed to be one of the arm-rest terminals from the throne of Alexander the Great (356-323 BC). Its pair is in the British Museum collection.

"Answers perfectly, never feeling too large: it is like dining in a great trunk, and you expect the lid to open."

6th Duke of Devonshire

Below: Sir Anthony van Dyck; *Portrait of Arthur Goodwin, M.P.* 1639

Above centre: Daniel Mytens; *Christian Bruce, Countess of Devonshire and her children, William, 3rd Earl of Devonshire, Charles and Anne, c.1629*

Above right: Anthony Nelme; *Pair of pilgrim bottles, 1715*

This dining room was used by the family whenever there were more than six people for dinner until the outbreak of World War II in 1939. Today it is used for a few exclusive formal dinners each year of up to forty people. The first dinner to have been held was for the Princess Victoria and her mother the Duchess of Kent in 1832. Victoria was 13-years-old and it was the first time she had dined formally in adult company. The 6th Duke was so anxious that it should go without fault that he held a full cooked rehearsal the night before.

The table is furnished with a *surtout de table* of silver. The two bottle-shaped containers were made by Anthony Nelme (?1672-1722) for the 3rd Earl of Burlington. The rest of the silver was commissioned by the 6th Duke from Paul Storr (1771-1844) and Robert Garrard (1793-1881), the country's leading silversmiths in the early 19th century. The *surtout* is a feature of *dining à la Russe*, the practice of dining with separate courses brought to you by a butler or footman, which was newly fashionable at this time.

The portraits were all brought from Devonshire House by the 6th Duke and set into fixed frames as part of the decoration of the walls. The large group portrait between the fireplaces shows Christian Bruce, Countess of Devonshire, with her sons, William and Charles, and her daughter, Anne, painted by Daniel Mytens (c.1590-before 1648). The eldest boy, on the left wearing the robes of the Order of the Bath, is the future 3rd Earl of Devonshire and was later painted by Sir Anthony van Dyck (1599-1641). That painting hangs to the right of the fireplace. Perhaps the finest portrait in the room is the full-length van Dyck of Sir Arthur Goodwin to the right of the door from the Dome Room. Between the windows are two early portraits by Frans Hals (1581-1666).

With the exception of the curtains and carpet, the room was originally conceived as a white and gold interior. The present red wall hangings were put up in 1996 at the same time as the original silk brocade curtains were rewoven. The chandelier and wall lights were added to the room in the 20th century.

"The Vestibule is well contrived, connected with the office staircase, and with spaces containing ovens, presses, and cupboards belonging to the dinner service."

6th Duke of Devonshire

The vestibule provided the gateway between the reception rooms and the domestic service offices and kitchens built for the 6th Duke. The door on the right as you enter from the Great Dining Room gives onto a staircase that connects to all the ground floor offices, including the Butler's Pantry, Servants Hall and Kitchen. Today these rooms are used as offices and workshops for the house. The area to the left acted as a servery and was originally fitted with cupboards for china and warming cupboards to help keep food hot before it was taken to the table.

The large chandelier was made in Germany to designs by Karl Fredrich Schinkel (1781-1841). The gilt bronze stags' heads were modelled by the sculptor Christian Rauch (1777-1857), and exhibit the naturalism that German sculpture was famous for at this time. The naturalism is enhanced further by the inclusion of real antlers, given to the 6th Duke by the King of Prussia. Above the chandelier is a gallery which was used for the performance of music whilst the guests ate in the Great Dining Room. On either side of the entrance to the servery are busts by Charles-Henri-Joseph Cordier (1827-1905) depicting Saïd Abdallah and the Venus Africaine. They were purchased by the 6th Duke from the Great Exhibition at the Crystal Palace in 1851.

In 2011 the New Gallery was created from some bedrooms in the adjacent corridor. It is now a temporary exhibition space which hosts a number of themed displays or loan exhibitions throughout the year.

Above: William Henry Hunt; *The Butler's Room, Chatsworth, 1823*

Right: William Henry Hunt; *The Kitchen, Chatsworth, c.1823*

"My Gallery was intended for modern sculpture, and I have almost entirely abstained from mixing it with any fragments of antiquity: It was in vain to hope for time or opportunities of collecting really fine ancient marbles."

6th Duke of Devonshire

At the time that the 6th Duke was creating this gallery, between 1818 and 1834, the fashion for collecting ancient sculpture which had dominated in the previous century meant that very few specimens were available for him to buy. Instead the 6th Duke's passion for marble sculpture led him to form a collection of early 19th-century European sculpture and it remains one of the most important in the world. Today the gallery is displayed as it was at the end of the 6th Duke's life.

The collection features works by some of the greatest sculptors of the time including: John Gibson (1786-1866), Rudolph Schadow (1786-1822), Lorenzo Bartolini (1777-1850), Michael von Schwanthaler (1802-1848) and Bertel Thorvaldsen (1770-1844). There are also six works by the most famous sculptor of the day, Antonio Canova (1757-1822), including the colossal bust of Napoleon in the centre of the gallery and the seated figure of Napoleon's mother Madame Mère. One of Canova's masterpieces, the figure of the sleeping shepherd Endymion with his dog, was a commission from the 6th Duke. In 1819 he asked Canova to make him a figure, but gave him no further instruction. The 6th Duke wanted the creative genius of the artist to be completely unrestrained, and Endymion is the result. The highly polished marble surface of the shepherd boy's skin represents the lustre of moonlight as he sleeps.

Above: Richard Keane; Photograph of the Sculpture Gallery, late 19th century

Top centre: Antonio Canova; Seated figure of Madame Mère (Letizia Ramolino), c.1846

Top left: Antonio Canova; Bust of Napoleon, c.1800s

Right: Antonio Canova; The Sleeping Endymion with his dog, 1822

One of the important inspirations for the gallery was the new top-lit Braccio Nuovo gallery in the Vatican in Rome. The 6th Duke wrote that he "admire[s] it extremely, and shall imitate much in a small scale at Chatsworth". His initial plan was to clad the walls of the Sculpture Gallery with richly coloured marbles, combined with a floor of Swedish porphyry, to create a similar effect to the Braccio Nuovo. The watercolour artist William Hunt (1790-1864) recorded a trial conducted with some of the sculptures, columns and vases in the Old Library in 1827.

The scheme was however abandoned in favour of the local gritstone used to build Chatsworth. This was for two reasons: firstly, the great expense of the coloured marbles, and secondly, the effect of reflected light. A number of the artists working for the 6th Duke advised him that the matt gritstone would create a better backdrop for the white statuary marble of the sculptures. Colour is still present in the gallery through the use of marble plinths and other objects, and marble table tops and panels inlaid with *pietra dura*.

This use of colour, together with the original arrangement of the sculptures according to the 6th Duke's plans, was recreated in 2009 following a two-year research project. The rearrangement was first prompted by the filming of *Pride and Prejudice* in 2004.

The 2009 representation revealed subtle narratives that existed in the placement of the sculptures. One of the most striking effects was the restoration of the lions at the end of the gallery to their original height so that they once more tower over visitors as they exit the gallery. The lions are copies after Canova's originals on the tomb of Pope Clement XIII (1693-1769) in St Peter's in the Vatican. The Chatsworth lions form a memorial of their own, placed either side of a great marble doorcase, overlooked by busts of Antonio Canova and the 6th Duke, artist and patron respectively, and creators of this gallery. The 6th Duke so admired Canova that he even acquired the artist's tools for sculpting clay models, placing them in the wall of the gallery in a small glass case like some venerated treasure.

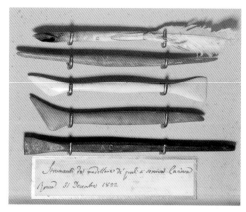

Top: Antonio Canova's Tools

Above: The Sculpture Gallery in 2002

Right: William Henry Hunt; Old Library, Chatsworth, c.1827

Opposite: Rinaldo Rinaldi, Sleeping Lion 1823-1825

Orangery, Chatsworth House

When originally conceived by Jeffry Wyatt, the 6th Duke's new suite of entertaining rooms on the garden front of the North Wing was intended to end at the Sculpture Gallery. Due to his new found enthusiasm for gardening, and encouraged by his head gardener and friend Joseph Paxton (1803-65), plans were made to add an Orangery, which would serve as the transition between house and garden.

Many prized tender plants flourished here, including four orange trees that had once belonged to Empress Josephine (1763-1814) at Malmaison. The large vase in the centre of the room, a copy by Lorenzo Bartolini (1777-1850) of the famous Medici Vase, is one of two original works of art to remain in the Orangery from the 6th Duke's time. The other being the central statue of Venus and Cupid by Cincinnati Baruzzi (1796-1878). He first placed the vase in the centre of the Sculpture Gallery, but quickly instructed for it

to go outside. On its journey to the garden it was placed temporarily in the Orangery and the Duke decided the effect was so beautiful it has remained here ever since. For evening entertainments he placed a series of powerful lamps inside the vase to project on the underside of the branches of the trees and plants, causing some of his guests to exclaim that it appeared like "fairyland".

In the early 1960s the first souvenirs, postcards and bon-bons were sold from a corner of the Orangery. In 1976 the Orangery was cleared and fitted out as a gift shop, although it was not until 1983 that the first Shop Manager was employed. Today, the Orangery Shop is one of four shops at Chatsworth selling a variety of gifts, souvenirs, garden and interior merchandise, as well as a small outlet which sells product from the Chatsworth Estate Farm Shop. These other shops are located in the stables.

The garden at Chatsworth consists of over 100 acres of diverse cultivation, the product of nearly 500 years of continual gardening on the site. Although many features and styles of gardening have been successively replaced to make way for new fashions, the garden retains vestiges of many earlier features and planting schemes.

The first garden was created by Sir William Cavendish and Bess of Hardwick in 1555. Much smaller than the garden today, it had a formal area to the south with ponds and fountains. Bess of Hardwick died in 1608, and little evidence survives of work carried out in the garden by her immediate successors, the 1st, 2nd and 3rd Earls of Devonshire. This changed dramatically after 1684 when the 4th Earl (later 1st Duke) inherited Chatsworth. In 1687 he began rebuilding the house, and the garden was developed to complement the palatial style of architecture. The 1st Duke was one of the first Englishmen to favour the extravagant creation of formal gardens which were already fashionable in France, Italy and Holland in the late 17th century.

The south parterre began construction in 1694 under the guidance of George London and Henry Wise, who also worked at Hampton Court Palace. The parterre was formed by symmetrical scrolled beds of flowers, formal clipped hedges and shrubs in planters and gravel paths. In very dry summers the pattern of paths can still be seen through the parched grass. The focal point of the parterre was a circular pool populated with a fountain of four sea horses and a Triton. The fountain still survives at the centre of the South Lawn. Carved by Caius Gabriel Cibber between 1688 to 1691, it is one of only two of the Baroque fountains to remain from the original total of nine.

Top: Johannes Kip after Leonard Knyff; Detail from an Engraving of Chatsworth, 1699

Middle: Samuel Watson; Sketch of a seahorse

Bottom: Detail of the Seahorse Fountain from a painting of Chatsworth in a private collection, late 17th century

The parterre and other formal terraces above were recorded by the artist and engraver Johannes Kip (1653-1722) and Leonard Knyff (1650-1721) as well as in a number of paintings. The formal terraces, fountains and gravel paths were replaced in the 18th century by the newly fashionable picturesque style of gardening.

The 2nd Duke made few changes to the garden he inherited in 1707. However, in 1728, the year before his death, initial attempts were made to simplify the geometric patterns of the 1st Duke's formal garden by levelling and turfing the south parterre. The 3rd and 4th Duke continued this work, probably advised by William Kent (1685-1748), who certainly produced designs for the remodelling of the cascade in a naturalistic manner. How much of the naturalisation of the garden was the result of William Kent, and how much was due to the involvement of Lancelot 'Capability' Brown (1716-1783) for the 4th Duke is not known.

Left: Archive photograph of the "Italian" garden

Right: The Canal Pond and South Front of Chatsworth House

All but three of the main fountains (those in the Ring Pond, the Canal, and the Sea Horse Fountain) were removed and their ponds filled in. Topiary and avenues disappeared, the terraces were levelled and replaced with grass, a 'ha-ha' was constructed to trick the eye into thinking the garden and park were continuous, and trees were planted in apparently natural clumps in both park and garden so there was no demarcation between the two. The 4th Duke's fundamental changes left the garden and park much as they appear today; after his death there followed almost half a century of inactivity.

In 1811 the 6th Duke inherited a garden which had been sadly neglected by his father. The restoration, on a very grand scale, was not immediate and 15 years were to pass before Joseph Paxton (1803-1865) was appointed as head gardener.

Paxton proved to be the most innovative garden designer of his era, and remains the greatest single influence on Chatsworth's garden. Traditionally known as the 'Pleasure Grounds' in the 19th century, the areas which extend away from the productive parts of the garden in the north-east corner behind the stables are dominated by his features, from the manmade rockery to the enclosed area of the Great Conservatory (demolished 1920), to the forty-acre Arboretum and eight-acre Pinetum of specimen trees.

The 7th and 8th Dukes made few changes, tending to maintain rather than develop the garden. In the 20th century the 9th and 10th Dukes both witnessed decline in the maintenance and development of the

garden. Two World Wars had the most drastic effect, as men joined up to fight and coal became rationed. The most significant casualty was the destruction of the Great Conservatory in 1920, which had become too costly to repair and maintain.

Following this period of austerity, the 11th Duke and Duchess Deborah decided the family should once more live at Chatsworth. From the early 1950s the garden began to undergo a renaissance under their management. Many new features were introduced, such as the Serpentine Hedge, Kitchen Garden and Display House, and the garden once more became a popular site of interest for visitors.

Right: Trough Waterfall

Bottom left: Henry Perronet Briggs; *Portrait of Sir Joseph Paxton*, 1836

Bottom right: Photograph of the Great Conservatory, 1890s

Opposite: View from the top of the Rock Garden

Below: A statue of Ceres (after the Antique)

Bottom left: A concert in the garden

Bottom right: Rose Garden

Improvements and developments to the garden continue today. Many of the historical features are being restored, such as the Sea Horse fountain, which after over 300 years in the Derbyshire climate was damaged and discoloured. Numerous plantings and borders are undergoing improvement, requiring the complete removal of old planting in many areas so that invasive weeds are eradicated prior to new plantings.

Work continues across the garden to improve and diversify the grass meadows. In many areas weed species and coarse grasses had dominated, resulting in little visual interest after the spring bulbs flower. Chemical control of the most aggressive species, extended and improved mowing regimes and the introduction of natural parasitic species such as yellow rattle help more interesting groups of plants to colonise.

In 2014 the garden designer Dan Pearson was commissioned to assist with the development of the twisting watercourse called the Trout Stream. Originally engineered by Paxton, the stream feeds water from Stand Wood above the garden to the Revelation fountain and pond and over the Wellington waterfall in the centre of Paxton's rockery. After initial clearance work along the stream sympathetic plantings will be introduced to give all-year-round interest and particularly spring colour.

At its peak in 1900 the gardens employed 60 full-time gardeners. Today it is maintained by a team of 20 gardeners, three full-time students and numerous volunteers, short-term trainees and work placements. It is open from the end of March to early January and can be enjoyed in all seasons. Highlights include spring colour with diverse bulb plantings, azaleas and rhododendron followed by summer bedding schemes and a rich show of autumn colour. The garden plays host to events throughout the year including sculpture exhibitions, concerts and theatre, garden parties and the firework displays in November.

BROAD WALK

"Sir Jeffry Wyatville's first great hit out of doors was the invention of the broad gravel walk that is of so much use and ornament here."

6th Duke of Devonshire

BROAD WALK

At just over half a kilometre (1740 feet) long and seven metres (23 feet) wide this is more of a road than a path. It was laid out adjacent to the 6th Duke's new North Wing and runs south under a canopy of beech trees that create a natural arched view like the column and vaulted space of a cathedral.

The path runs from Flora's Temple at the north to a large stone urn inscribed in memory of 'Blanche'. Blanche Georgiana Howard was a much adored niece of the 6th Duke and married William Cavendish who succeeded as 7th Duke in 1858. Sadly Blanche died very young in 1840; the 6th Duke was heart-broken and placed the vase in this prominent position as a permanent memorial to her.

FLORA'S TEMPLE

Originally called the Bowling Green House, Flora's Temple was built between 1693 and 1695. Kip and Knyff's engraving shows it standing, beside the bowling-green to the south-west of the house. The temple was moved to its present site in 1750. The sculptor Jan Nost (d.1729) carved the statue of Flora in 1694 and it is one of the few sculptures that survive from the 1st Duke's garden. Most of the other sculptures from this time have been lost, or were relocated such as those which decorate the Great Stairs inside the house.

The temple also houses the skeleton trunks of the two *Camellia reticulata* 'Captain Rawes' that grew in the centre of the Case which runs the length of the Conservative Wall adjacent to the temple from c.1840. These camellias died of old age in 2000 and 2002. Captain Rawes served in the Honourable East India Company and brought the first *Camellia reticulata* plant to this country in 1820. The plant was subsequently named 'Captain Rawes' in his honour and it remained the only known *Camellia reticulata* cultivated in Europe for over a century. The two plants growing in the Case today were propagated from the original plants in 1988.

THE CASE

The Case acts as a protective cover for the tender plants grown inside it. Originally called the Conservative Wall and designed by Joseph Paxton in 1838, it is backed by an ingenious system of flues and hot water pipes, to keep the temperature high enough in the winter for half-hardy plants to grow successfully. Initially, there were projecting wooden panels from which canvas curtains were hung to prevent the fruit blossom from being damaged by frost. In 1848 Paxton covered it with the wood and glass structure.

The Case is 91 metres (300 feet) long and protects, peaches, nectarines, apricots and various shrubs from the unpredictable Derbyshire climate.

Top: Flora's Temple

Middle: Johannes Kip after Leonard Knyff; Detail of the Bowling Green House from an Engraving of Chatsworth 1699

Bottom: Caius Gabriel Cibber; Detail of a Figure of Flora, 1687-99

Right: Hand coloured photograph of the Conservative Wall, 19th century

WEATHER STATION

Daily fluctuations in the weather have been noted at Chatsworth more or less continuously since the 18th century. To indulge this interest in the weather, there has been a weather station on the Salisbury Lawns for many years. The rain gauge is measured and emptied every day and there is an ingenious method for recording the hours of sunshine in the form of a Campbell-Stokes Sunshine Recorder. The small glass sphere is designed to focus the rays from the sun onto a card mounted at the back and is set on a stand. The burn marks on the card show when and for how long the sun shone on any given day. The Stevenson Screen holds thermometers which record daily minimum, maximum and ambient temperatures.

SALISBURY LAWNS

The lawn to the east of the house, presumably named after the Salisbury Plain in Wiltshire, is divided by a broad gravel path running east/west from the bottom of the Cascade to the Broad Walk. The lawn on the north side is called Great Salisbury (just less than three acres), while the lawn on the south side is called Little Salisbury (just over two and a half acres).

The lawns most likely date to the 1730s during the time of the 3rd Duke, possibly under advice from William Kent who advocated laying out gardens in a less formal, more natural way, as he achieved in the early modifications at Stowe House in Buckinghamshire.

In 1983, Dr O.I. Gilbert from the University of Sheffield wrote an article describing the rich variety of grasses, mosses, sedges and wildflowers growing in the Salisbury Lawns. In light of these findings no weed killers or fertilisers are ever used and the only maintenance carried out on these 280 year old lawns is mowing.

Opposite: William Cowen; View of Chatsworth from the South East with a rainbow, 1828

Top left: View of the Salisbury Lawn and the North Wing of Chatsworth

Above: The Weather Station

1st DUKE'S GREENHOUSE

The 1st Duke's Greenhouse of the 1690s was a long, low building, with ten arched windows. Its original site was at the north end of the Broad Walk, in almost the same position as Flora's Temple and The Case now stand. It fronted on to a rectangular pond larger than the footprint of the house, which had a tall single jet of water at its centre. In the 1760s the 4th Duke re-sited the greenhouse, somewhat modified, to its present site. Today it overlooks the Rose Garden and has been enriched with the addition in the 1830s of carved stone brackets and busts, which originally formed part of the 1st Duke's decoration of the courtyard in the centre of the house.

Greenhouses were first developed in Holland at the start of the 17th century taking their name from their original use to house tender greens, or evergreens, during the winter. They were also often referred to as orangeries because they were used in particular to grow citrus species and similar plants.

The 1st Duke's Greenhouse (which is open to visitors), is one of the most important 17th-century greenhouses to survive in England. It now houses part of the large Camellia collection, as well as various climbers that require protection from the frost.

Below: Camellia x williamsii 'Water Lily'

> *"We have decided to leave this currently unfashionable rose garden as it was laid out by my grandmother, as a generational 'layer'. The yew hedges provide welcome shelter though we have removed the hedge on the south side to improve the views inwards and outwards."*
>
> 12th Duke of Devonshire

ROSE GARDEN

In 1939 Duchess Mary, wife of the 10th Duke, remodelled the area in front of the 1st Duke's Greenhouse, enclosed it with a yew hedge and planted hybrid tea roses. Over the years the plants and soil have been replaced and various edging plants have been used. Today the 16 rose beds are edged with catmint (*Nepeta x faassenii*).

The four central flower beds are planted with *Phlox* 'White Admiral', which flowers later than the roses, therefore extending the season of interest. These four beds are edged with alpine strawberries. The flower beds immediately in front of the 1st Duke's Greenhouse are home to a collection of tree peonies, which flower from April to mid-June.

CASCADE

One of the most popular features in the garden is the Cascade. It was designed by Grillet, a French hydraulics engineer with experience in designing decorative waterworks for Louis XIV, King of France (1638-1715) at the Chateau du Marly near Versailles. It took two years to construct and was completed in 1696. No sooner was it complete than the 1st Duke was already contemplating enlarging it.

In 1702 this masterpiece of a water amusement was torn up, and replaced with a longer, steeper flight than before. At the top a new temple was built, the Cascade House, designed by Thomas Archer (1668-1743) to deliver water to the cascade in increasingly dramatic ways. The stone nymphs were recycled from the original scheme and added to with Dolphins and a figure of Fluvius, carved by Henri Nadauld (1653-1723). In addition, elements of surprise were introduced, such as the jets set into the floor of the temple which "throw up several stream and wett people"

as recorded in 1725. These jets still exist in the floor today. The remodelling was largely completed by 1708 and work on the supply pond, the Cascade Pond, which is sited higher up the hill, continued until 1712. The new Cascade was nearly twice the length and substantially wider than its predecessor.

All the water which runs down the Cascade feeds the Sea Horse fountain in the south lawn, from where the water continues in a pipe into the river Derwent.

Opposite: Designed by William Kent, Stone Herm, 1725-1749

RING POND

This circular pond remains from the 1st Duke's garden where the Squirting Willow Tree stood on the island in the centre. The current lead duck fountain (1693) was moved from a now filled in pond at the north side of the Cascade in the 1960s.

Around the outer hedges are a number of herms (stone heads on tapering posts) which were designed by William Kent in the 18th century and were only placed here in 1893. They originally stood in the gardens at Chiswick House in west London.

SERPENTINE HEDGES

In 1953, the Serpentine Hedges were planted, an idea which Duchess Deborah took from the 'crinkle-crankle' wall at Hopton Hall near Wirksworth. At the same time, the semi-circle of beech hedging around the lower half of the Ring Pond was planted to create a complete circle begun by Duchess Evelyn half a century before.

"Paxton invented an 'apparatus' on which the vast stones were moved and winched into place."

Duchess Deborah

Below: the Wellington Rock

ROCK GARDEN AND STRID

The Rockery was built as a reminder of the 6th Duke's visit to the Alps during his Grand Tour of Europe. Work began in 1842 and the stone was brought from Dobb Edge, north of Stand Wood. The largest construction, the Wellington Rock, is 14 metres (45 feet) high and has a waterfall running down it. There is a maze of paths threading round and beneath the rocks.

Work also began in 1842 on the excavation of the 'Bolton Stride' or Strid. This was based on a real feature - the narrow chasm cut by the river Wharfe - on the Devonshire's Bolton Abbey Estate in Yorkshire.

In 2002-2003, partial restoration was undertaken on the much collapsed higher rockery. At the same time a viewing platform was established with views west across the Strid, over the Ring Pond and Serpentine Hedge, into the Park beyond.

In 2007, the Duchess planted a collection of dark or black flowers in a border called the Dark Side, at the northern entrance to the Rock Garden.

WILLOW TREE FOUNTAIN

The Willow Tree Fountain is an 'artificial tree of brass' originally created by an engineer called Ibeck in 1695. It was first placed in the centre of the Ring Pond and has been remade twice.

The present-day fountain is an early 19th-century version to replace the original which had become decayed. It was made by Bowers of Chesterfield who undertook the work for the 6th Duke. In 1844, the Willow Tree Fountain was relocated to its present site at the northern edge of the Rockery, in a small glade behind a collection of Paxton's rocks. It is now in need of restoration.

Above: Photograph of the Willow Tree Fountain, 1899

"Its success has been complete, both for the growth of plants and enjoyment it affords, being, I believe, the only hothouse known, to remain in which longer than ten minutes does not produce a state of fatigue."

6th Duke of Devonshire

GREAT CONSERVATORY

Paxton's Great Conservatory took four years to build and was completed in 1840. The building was 84 metres (275 feet) long, 37 metres (121 feet) wide and 19 metres (62 feet) high, the largest glass building in England. This was the forerunner of Paxton's subsequent masterpiece, the Crystal Palace in London erected in 1851. Inside the Great Conservatory there was room for two carriages to pass on the main thoroughfare and stairs, hidden by ascending rocks, led to a gallery from which you could inspect the highest branches of the exotic palms and other trees that flourished there. There were ponds full of aquatic plants, rocks, mosses, ferns and brilliantly coloured flowers in a tropical climate.

To create this climate there were eight underground boilers fuelled by coal which arrived by wagons through underground tunnels. The boilers fed a seven mile maze of 15 centimetre (six inch) hot-water pipes. The boiler fumes escaped through flues laid along the ground to a chimney up in Stand Wood, well out of sight of the garden.

During and after the First World War (1914-1918) there was insufficient coal to heat the conservatory and many of the plants died. Because of the expense of restoring the now semi-derelict building and in view of the huge cost of maintaining and heating it, the Great Conservatory was demolished in 1920. Only the supporting walls were left as a lasting memorial to this extraordinary building.

MAZE

Occupying the site of Paxton's Great Conservatory, this garden is now home to a large yew maze designed by Denis Fisher, when Comptroller at Chatsworth, in 1962 for the 11th Duke. 1209 English common yews *Taxus baccata* were planted to create it.

In the 1920s flower beds were laid out at each end within the remaining walls of the Great Conservatory with paths through and around them. The planting changes but the beds remain. At the north end herbaceous borders frame four central beds and at the south end a more intricate pattern of beds are filled with *Dahlia* in the summer and bulbs for spring interest.

COAL HOLE & TUNNEL

The Coal Hole to the north-east of the Great Conservatory is out of sight of the main path through the Rockery. Horse-drawn carts carrying coal, entered the garden above the stables and took the track under the Cascade and on to the Coal Hole. From here the coal was taken in small wagons along the underground railway.

Parts of the tunnel had become blocked since the destruction of the Great Conservatory. Filming at Chatsworth encouraged an exploratory dig in 2002. Clearing the tunnel and coal hole revealed that it had been filled in with rubbish including plants and pots from the time that the Great Conservatory was destroyed. After the tunnel was excavated, the tracks were removed and handrails and lighting were installed. The Coal Hole and Tunnel opened to visitors in 2003.

CONNER GROVE

In 2011, a glade to the west of Bamboo Walk opened and a collection of portrait busts by Angela Conner (b.1935) were installed there. The collection at Chatsworth includes portrait busts of various public figures and members of the 12th Duke's family; Lady Emma Tennant, Harold Macmillan, Sir Tom Stoppard, Lord Rothschild, Sir Roy Strong, Sir Patrick Leigh Fermor, Sir John Betjeman, Andrew, 11th Duke of Devonshire, Deborah, Duchess of Devonshire, HM The Queen, HRH The Prince of Wales, Lucian Freud and the Earl of Burlington.

HUNDRED STEPS

The Hundred Steps were created in the 1980s. This long straight ascent runs uphill from the Maze and is aligned on its centre. Halfway along it is interrupted by a lone *Araucaria araucana* (monkey puzzle). A Greek Altar has been put at the top of the steps, on the Arboretum Walk.

Top left: Hundred Steps

Left: Coal Tunnel

Above: Angela Conner; Portrait busts of Deborah Duchess of Devonshire, 2004 and Sir Patrick Leigh Fermor, 1973

CANAL POND AND THE GREAT FOUNTAIN

The Canal Pond was dug between 1702 and 1703. Its construction involved the removal of Flora's Garden, shown to the south of the great parterre on the Kip and Knyff engraving (p75). The Canal Pond is set a few inches higher than the South Lawn which creates the illusion that the house appears to rise out of the water when viewed from the furthest end of the canal.

There has been a fountain playing at the north end of the Canal since the pond was completed. Named the Great Fountain, it is flanked by two river gods, attributed to the sculptor Nadauld. The jet nozzle of the Great Fountain can still be seen in the foreground, but in 1844 it was superseded by the Emperor Fountain designed by Joseph Paxton.

On the bank of the Canal Pond is the sculpture Cornwall Slate Line (1990) by Richard Long (b.1945). Many of his works are inspired by walks through nature and the countryside, and he is closely associated with the artform Land Art. The majority of his works have been made to be displayed with the landscape they have been inspired by.

Above: Richard Long, Cornwall Slate Line, 1990

Right: J.C. Bourne; Engraved view of the Emperor Fountain, c.1850

"the Emperor Fountain is the spirit of novelty, dashing its endless variety to the skies."

6th Duke of Devonshire

EMPEROR FOUNTAIN

When it became known that Tsar Nicholas I (1796-1855), Emperor of Russia, was to visit Chatsworth in 1844, the idea of welcoming the Tsar with a fountain even higher than that at Peterhof (the Tsar's palace in north-east Russia) appealed to the 6th Duke. Although the Great Fountain, installed by the 1st Duke, was the highest in this country, the 6th Duke put Paxton's engineering skills into action to create a new record-breaking gravity-fed fountain.

Sadly the Tsar never visited Chatsworth, but the new fountain was still named after him. It is on record as having reached the height of 90 metres (295 feet). It is powered only by the pressure of water dropping 122 metres (397 feet), through a 40cm diameter cast-iron pipe. It was the tallest gravity fed fountain in the world for 160 years.

The main elements of the system have been recently refurbished and a new bronze nozzle

has been fitted to the fountain. It is believed that Paxton originally used different nozzles to create a variety of water effects as well as to achieve greater height.

Today the fountain operates from the small bypass valve. Despite the narrower gauge of the bypass a height of 62 metres (200 feet) can still be achieved on a still day.

Allen Jones; Déjeuner sur l'Herbe , 2007

Photograph of Dennis Penrose and his wife walking in the Ravine, 1935

RAVINE AND AZALEA DELL

One of the few areas to see development in the early 20th century was the Ravine and Azalea Dell. In the early 1930s, the 9th Duke's wife Duchess Evelyn, in collaboration with the head gardener, J. G. Weston, created the Ravine and the Azalea Dell in the south of the garden. These areas of planting were in the woodland garden fashion as promoted by William Robinson and Gertrude Jekyll who favoured wild or natural gardens over traditional formal gardens.

The area was neglected during World War II becoming overgrown and lacking interest. Recently, work has been carried out to restore and revive the Ravine. The path now meanders across the stream in several places and the pools have been enlarged. As is the case throughout the garden, the *Rhododendron ponticum* has been removed as a precaution to stop the spread of the disease *Phytophthera ramorum*. As a result the now bare steep banks of the Ravine have been planted with many trees and shrubs which will mature and fill the area with new colour and interest.

Twice a year the shrubs in the Azalea Dell give a spectacular display of colour. In late May the solid mass of blooms of the Double Ghent azaleas and *Rhododendron luteum* combine to give a heady aroma, and in the autumn the leaves produce a second colourful display.

QUEBEC

In 2008 the 12th Duke and Duchess re-established Quebec, a long-overgrown area of garden below the Canal Pond. (The 9th Duke may have named this area on his return to Chatsworth having served as Governor General of Canada.) Following the clearance that year a cascade overflow from the Canal Pond dating from the early 1700s was revealed.

The sculpture *Déjeuner sur l'Herbe* was commissioned for the site at the south end of Quebec in 2006-2007. The work by Allen Jones (b.1937) features three seated figures picnicking and looking out over the Old Park. The subject is a modern interpretation of the famous Impressionist painting by Édouard Manet.

Cascade overflow from the Canal Pond

GROTTO POND & MORTON POND

The Grotto Pond was probably created around 1700, a similar time to the Morton Pond which was designed to supply the Great Fountain in the 1st Duke's new Canal Pond.

The 5th Duke (1748-1811) added the Grotto. This was originally constructed in the late 1790s at the instigation of his wife Duchess Georgiana but was much altered by the 6th Duke in the 1820s. It is built of massive boulders and the chamber is surmounted by a rustic timber bandstand with a conical slate roof.

TROUGH WATERFALL

In 1992 the overflow from the stream leaving the Grotto Pond was turned into a water feature, the Trough Waterfall, using a series of stone agricultural drinking troughs gathered from the nearby fields and farms.

The Drummer, 1989-1990 by Barry Flanagan (1941-2009) is situated at the north end of the Grotto Pond, at the base of grass path up a steep bank. Bought by the 12th Duke to celebrate his and his wife's move when they came to live at Chatsworth.

Top left: Barry Flanagan; Drummer, 2004

Top right: Grotto

Left: Trough Waterfall

"This is probably my favourite part of the garden: it is always peaceful, even on the busiest days and, as well as the magnificent trees it has the best views out over Lancelot Brown's landscape."

Duchess of Devonshire

PINETUM

In the early to mid-19th-century important developments in British gardening took place. Gardens continued to develop in their complexity, scale and importance; at this time there was a growing interest in scientific horticulture. New plants from the Americas, Africa and Asia had arrived in Britain in increasing numbers during the 18th century, but scientific plant-hunting expeditions, many of which the 6th Duke sponsored, were becoming increasingly commonplace.

The Pinetum was created between 1830 and 1831, established from eight acres added to the garden from the Old Park. Here the 6th Duke and Paxton indulged their passion for collecting on a grand scale. This was one of the first pinetums, or collections of coniferous trees, in England. It includes *Cedrus libani* (Lebanon cedar), *Picea* (spruce), *Pseudotsuga menziesii* (Douglas fir), *Larix* (Larch), *Sequoiadendron giganteum* (giant redwood), *Araucaria araucana* (monkey puzzle) and *Pinus parviflora* (Japanese white pine).

During the stormy winter of 2013-2014 several of Paxton's specimens were destroyed. These losses have prompted a thorough review of the management of the Pinetum. An up-to-date survey of what trees are growing where and as much of their history as can be established from the archive has been undertaken. In the autumn of 2014 a programme of

re-stocking some of Paxton's key introductions began together with the addition of other softwoods. It is hoped that the Pinetum can be expanded to enable the addition of more specimens.

In 2006 the sculpture *Forms that Grow in the Night* was commissioned from David Nash (b.1947) by the Duke and Duchess. It is a site-specific work for Chatsworth, and together they selected the site at the south end of the Pinetum. The three shapes are formed from two fallen oak trees from Sussex, which were carved and then charred at the artist's studio. They were brought to Chatsworth and installed at the end of April 2009. Once installed the artist charred them again and sprayed linseed oil over the blackened wood. This ensures a much longer life than if the wood was left untreated.

Top left: Joseph Hooker; *Larix griffithii* from *Illustrations of Himalayan plants*, London 1855

Bottom left: View of the Park from the Pinetum

Right: David Nash; Forms that Grow in the Nights, 2008-2009

"We take this two mile walk very often. Along it we are creating different areas of horticultural interest based on various genus of plants: 'Cornus Corner', 'Viburnum Valley' and so on. Each area is also planned to have a good view and a comfortable seat."

12th Duke of Devonshire

ARBORETUM WALK, TROUT STREAM AND SPECTACLES

Begun in 1835, the Arboretum was one of Paxton's greatest contributions to the Chatsworth landscape, a succession of trees systematically planted in accordance by their botanical classification. Its creation was a vast enterprise, involving among other things the diversion, along the Trout Stream, of a natural stream for more than two miles from its original course on the East Moor, in order to provide a picturesque element in the design.

Few traces of the original planting survive, and what is called the Arboretum today is the eastern area of the garden where trees and shrubs dominate. As in the rest of the garden, the area has recently been cleared of *Rhododendron ponticum* revealing many new views. Plantings have been increased and groups of *Magnolia, Eucryphia* and *Acer* amongst many others add interest.

SUMMER HOUSE & GOLDEN GROVE

On Holly Walk, the path above the Summer House, is a collection of hollies which were planted by Duchess Deborah. *Ilex aquifolium* 'Flavescens', 'Madame Briot', 'Bacciflava', 'Silver van Tol', 'Ferox Argentea', and 'Handsworth New Silver' are planted in big groups, interspersed with *Araucaria araucana* (monkey puzzle).

The Summer House was described by the 6th Duke, he wrote: 'here is, or ought to be, Luttrell's seat, in the spot he fancied: the style is Saracenic; the columns are of Aberdeen granite, and the rude central capital of serpentine came with me from Palermo, and is the cause of this manner of decoration.'

Near the Summer House is an area planted in gold and yellow - the Golden Grove. All the shrubs and small trees here were given by friends and neighbours of the 11th Duke and Duchess to mark their golden wedding anniversary in 1991. Planting includes *Acer shirasawanum* 'Aureum', *Rhododendron* 'Haida Gold' and 'Golden Wedding' and *Spiraea x japonica* 'Goldflame' and 'Gold Mound'.

Above the Golden Grove is a densely planted area of mixed shrubs including *Viburnum, Hydrangea* and *Enkianthus*. Here the Trout Stream meanders along the path before tumbling over a rocky cascade and disappearing underground from where it feeds the Revelation Pond and Wellington Waterfall.

Opposite: Stone garden urn on the Green Drive

Left: Trout Stream

KITCHEN GARDEN

Chatsworth has grown its own food for centuries, and the kitchen gardens have had various sites over the years, but recently they were moved to the east of the stables. This ground was originally called the paddocks because it was where the carriage horses were turned out to graze.

The 11th Duke and Duchess established these gardens because the Duchess was very enthusastic to create an ornamental kitchen garden, a feature lacking in the garden at Chatsworth.

It was redesigned during the winters of 1991-1992 and 1992-1993. New drainage was laid, raised beds were built from old bricks, and some new paths were bordered with railway sleepers. Iron arches were installed to support fruit trees.

Many different varieties of fruit, salad, flowers for cutting and vegetables are grown here, including 'mummy peas', thought to have grown from peas discovered in Tutankhamun's tomb in 1922. The house

is supplied with produce from the kitchen garden and surplus is sold in the Stable Yard and Chatsworth Estate Farm Shop.

Beyond a beech hedge at the lower part of the garden is a small orchard, where local varieties of apples are grown, including 'Beeley Pippin' which was raised by Reverend C. Sculthorpe in the estate village of Beeley around 1880.

REVELATION

This water powered flower, installed in 1999, has four huge petals of stainless steel that open and close around a central gold sphere every five minutes. It was designed and built by Angela Conner (b.1935) a friend of the family and the artist responsible for the bronze heads sited within the garden near the Ravine.

COTTAGE GARDEN

The Cottage Garden was created in 1989, based on a design exhibited at Chelsea Flower Show by the Women's Institute. It consists of topiary 'rooms' and 'furniture' created out of box, privet and yew. There is a formal 'front garden' containing beds framed by box with changing seasonal colourful displays. To the rear are vegetable plots with apple arches across the central path, these plots are designed, planted and managed by garden trainees every year

SENSORY GARDEN

The Sensory Garden was created in 2003, in conjunction with Lord Burlington, the 12th Duke's son. Plants were chosen for their impact on the five senses - sight, smell, touch, hearing and taste. The paths are constructed using materials with different textures and wind chimes add an extra element to the experience of sound.

Opposite top: The Rotary Diamond in the Kitchen Garden

Opposite bottom right: Laura Ellen Bacon; Woven Form 2012

Top left: Angela Conner; Revelation, 1999

Top right: Cottage Garden

Above: Sensory Garden

VINERY

Built about 1834, this is the sole survivor of three glasshouses constructed specifically for orchids by Joseph Paxton. It contained the 6th Duke's superb collection, gathered from all over the world. Several orchids were named after Chatsworth, Paxton or the 6th Duke e.g. *Coelogyne cristata* 'Chatsworth', *Dendrobium paxtonii*, and *Stanhopea devoniensis*.

It now houses white peaches, Camellias, and Royal Horticultural Society prize winning dessert grapes *Vitis* 'Muscat of Alexandria', which were mostly planted in the 1920s.

Below: Joseph Paxton; *Cymbiduim devonianum*, from the Magazine of Botany, and Register of Flowering Plants, London 1834-49

Right: Interior of the Vinery with 'Muscat of Alexandria' grapes

SNAKE TERRACE

In 1974 the Snake Terrace was constructed in the space between the 1st Duke's Greenhouse and the Display House. This, like the maze, was designed by Denis Fisher using wedge-shaped stone taken from Paxton's old Lily House on the Estate. The serpent motif (the crest of the Cavendish family) is picked out in pebbles taken from the beach at Eastbourne in Sussex, a town the family helped to expand and develop as a tourist destination in the 19th century.

The terrace was linked to Paxton's Case by the Laburnum Arch in 1974 which from late spring is a mass of yellow scented racemes. The leaves, flowers and seeds of laburnum are poisonous.

DISPLAY GREENHOUSE

This greenhouse, built in 1970, is sited behind the 1st Duke's Greenhouse. It has three climatic zones, Tropical, Mediterranean and Temperate. In 2011, the Temperate and Mediterranean Zones were opened to visitors for the first time; however the Tropical Zone is not open to visitors in order to prevent the loss of heat and humidity.

In the Temperate Zone, which is kept no lower than 4°C, early blooming *Camellia, Rhododendron, Clianthus, Acacia,* and other plants from mild climates are grown.

The Mediterranean Zone, where the minimum temperature is 13°C, houses oranges, lemons, limes, and loquats, which thrive there. Two or three times in the summer a night flowering cactus (*Epiphyllum* species), flowers for just a single night producing up to 80 flowers, 30cm across.

In the far left corner of the Mediterranean Zone is a *Citrus limone* 'Imperial'. This is a cross between lemon and grapefruit producing large yellow fruit. The Imperial

Lemon is used in the house to make marmalade. In 2012 it won first prize in the Miscellaneous Glasshouse Fruit category in the Royal Horticultural Society Autumn Fruit and Vegetable Competition.

The final, tropical section, that can be viewed through the glass division, is maintained to a minimum temperature of 16°C, only 3°C more than the Mediterranean. In each corner is a banana plant, *Musa acuminata* 'Dwarf Cavendish'. This was imported from Mauritius in 1829, and did so well at Chatsworth that Paxton sent one to Samoa with John Williams, a missionary. There it flourished and is now the largest commercially grown banana in the world.

In the central pond is the water-lily, *Victoria amazonica*. Paxton acquired a plant from Kew where it had failed to flower, and in a specially constructed glasshouse (now destroyed) Paxton managed to produce the first flower in this country in 1849. The lily is an annual and, if possible, is grown each year from seed collected by the glasshouse team from the pond after flowering.

Top left: The Display Greenhouse

Above top: Dwarf banana *Musa acuminata* 'Cavendishii' in the Display greenhouse

Above bottom: William Jackson Hooker and Walter Fitch; The Victoria Regia Lily from Illustrations of the Royal Waterlily of South America , London 1851

"...at the top of a considerable eminence, where the wood ceased, and the eye was instantly caught by Pemberley House, situated on the opposite side of a valley, into which the road with some abruptness wound. It was a large, handsome stone building, standing well on rising ground, and backed by a ridge of high woody hills; and in front a stream of some natural importance was swelled into greater, but without artificial appearance. Elizabeth was delighted. She had never seen a place for which nature had done more, or where natural beauty had been so little counteracted by an awkward taste."

Jane Austen, Pride and Prejudice

The park creates the setting for the house and garden, and is enjoyed by many thousands in its own right.

Following the purchase of land at Chatsworth in 1549 by Sir William Cavendish and Bess of Hardwick, the area east and north of the house was cultivated to produce food such as fruit. The deer park, to the east of the house, was established to provide venison, with the Stand Tower on the hill behind the house built to observe the hunt. In the valley, ponds were created off the river Derwent to manage the fish stocks.

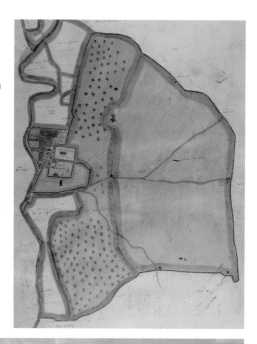

Opposite: William Marlow; *A view of Chatsworth*, c.1770

Top right: William Senior; Chatsworth from the Survey of the Estates of the 1st and 2nd Earls of Devonshire c.1610-1627

Right: Richard Wilson A view of Elizabethan Chatsworth (detail), 1740-1749

The development of the wider park was gradual until the 4th Duke engaged Lancelot 'Capability' Brown (1716-1783) in the 1760s to change the main views into and out from the house and dramatically change the approach. Brown's foreman, Michael Milliken (d.1800), oversaw the expansion and beautification of the park by incorporating previously enclosed fields to the west of the river and removing completely from view the village of Edensor.

Under the 6th Duke improvements to the park continued, most noticeably at the new site for Edensor, where houses were built or remodelled in numerous styles of architecture with the intention of creating a romantic country village. Along the main road from the gated entrance to the new model village two picturesque gate-lodges were also built where the main road enters the Park.

In the late 19th century the Park became a popular destination for day trippers from the increasingly industrialised towns which surround the Peak District. This popularity continued into the 20th century, and today the Park welcomes over one million visitors a year.

The Park now covers 400 hectares and is enclosed by a 14.5 kilometre (nine-mile) stone wall and deer fence. The majority is accessible to the public.

Since the 19th century the Domain (or Park) Team manage the landscape. This requires a delicate balance between preserving and enhancing the designed landscape, maintaining standards of presentation and ensuring the protection of the ecological habitat. Work includes many aspects which go unseen, such as maintaining and repairing kilometres of pipes and stone drains (known locally as soughs), which move water around the site supplying the gravity-fed fountains in the garden and draining the grassland in the valley to the river.

and to ensure the minimum impact of events, the ground is well drained, the grass is kept in good condition, and in areas where car parking is frequently necessary a reinforcing mesh has been added to the ground.

The Old Park is a 'Site of Special Scientific Interest' and provides a sanctuary for deer and other wildlife and consequently cannot be open to the public. It contains nearly four hundred veteran trees, probably over five hundred years old, and provides a unique habitat for invertebrates and fungi.

Livestock are grazed across the Park, which is part of a working farm. It is stocked with sheep, cattle, and red and fallow deer. The livestock ensure the grassland is controlled and create the distinctive grazing line that can be seen under the canopies of trees. As part of the management of the livestock, boundary walls are continually repaired and maintained.

The Park also provides a venue for many and varied events throughout the year, from charity walks to large-scale concerts, as well as the annual International Horse Trials in the Spring and the Chatsworth Country Fair in the Autumn. To safeguard the Park for the future,

Opposite:
Top: View from the Hunting Tower

Middle: Edensor

Bottom: View through the columns of the Belvedere

Top: Limousin cattle

Above left: Fallow deer in the Park

Centre: the Country Fair

Above right: The Old Park

THE PARK MANAGEMENT PLAN

In 2012 a Park Management Plan was commissioned in a partnership between Chatsworth House Trust, Peak District National Park Authority, Natural England and English Heritage. The plan included in-depth research and surveying of the Park to create a comprehensive archive of its condition and attributes. The management plan gives a clear evolution of the Park, and its most important aspects and features. It includes a long-term management strategy for the future, with a wide range of recommendations. In 2014 implementation of these recommendations began, made possible in part by funding from Natural England.

An important aspect of the management of the Park is the controlled removal of trees. Tree felling is only carried out where a tree is un-healthy, incorrectly positioned or of an unsuitable species. In some areas tree removals will restore Brown's original intention for views through the landscape, which have been lost as newer plantings mature. Inappropriate species of trees for the date or appearance of an area of the Park will also be removed. In the future this will extend to the management of the skyline, which is currently dominated by the spikes of forestry conifers planted in the 20th century. It is intended that with time a natural, semi-native woodland, will again dominate. In addition new plantings are being introduced to better frame views, introduce young healthy stock, or replace failing trees.

Important landmarks and eye-catchers in the Park are being restored and conserved. This includes the built features such as the Golden Gates, Game Larder and Paine's Mill. Boundary walls and fences will be re-built or upgraded to ensure the park is secure, and where appropriate historic ditches or ha-has and aesthetic park fencing will be added.

To prevent erosion and failure of the banks along the River Derwent re-enforcing works will be undertaken at key points. Stone or timber structures will re-establish the line of the bank with a backfill of soil, re-creating Brown's intention including the broad area of water opposite the house, whilst observing and enhancing the ecological presence along the river.

Below right: Blueprint of the Game Larder, 1909

Bottom: Photograph of the Golden Gates, 1950s

Opposite: *William Cowen; View of Chatsworth from the west, 1828*

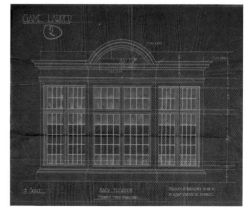

> *"It seems strange that this apparently perfect and wild backdrop to the house is only two or three hundred years old. In Bess of Hardwick's time it was a bare and rocky escarpment but I hope that the tree cover remains, it seems perfect."*
>
> 12th Duke of Devonshire

Below left: William Kent; Design for Cascade at Chatsworth, 1735-1740

Below right: Photograph of the Aqueduct when frozen, 1920s

STAND WOOD

Stand Wood covers a steep escarpment behind the house, formed of a grit stone edge that is visible in places on the surface as very large boulders. Some boulders were probably used to form the rockery in the garden in the mid-19th century.

When Chatsworth was acquired in 1549 the site of the wood was bare except for a number of parkland trees, and the ancient oaks that still stand within the wood date from this time. The area was the original deer park and the Stand or Hunting Tower was built in the mid-16th century to provide a view of the hunt, and a place to entertain the family and visiting guests.

Referring to the then bare, unwooded hillside Charles Cotton described Chatsworth in 1681 in his *Wonders of the Peak* as how a "…bright diamond would look, if set in a vile socket of ignoble jet." In the mid-18th century the area was planted with mixed woodland to provide a softer landscape backdrop to the house, probably suggested by either William Kent (1685-1748) for the 3rd Duke, or later as part of Lancelot Brown's work for the 4th Duke. It was at this time that it became known as Stand Wood as a reference to the tower.

Four man-made lakes collect water on a plateau immediately above the wood and supply all of the garden fountains, and also provide for garden watering, flushing toilets, and the fire-hydrant system. Water from here is also directed to generate electricity via the Turbine House. Emperor Lake is the largest of the four and was engineered by Sir Joseph Paxton (1803-1865) in 1844 to supply a new gravity fed fountain in the Canal Pond, the Emperor Fountain. The lake is

filled by over 4 kilometres (2½ miles) of streams that spread across the moorland. The three other lakes are earlier in date, created for the nine fountains and the Cascade that existed in the 1st Duke's garden of the 1690s.

In the mid-19th century the 6th Duke and Paxton added further planting, including exotic specimens, and enhanced the dramatic rock formations. New water features were also added by them as part of the lake and stream system, most notably the Aqueduct fed by water over the naturally occurring Sowter Stone. At the same time new footpaths and drives were established, and the ornamental Swiss Cottage was constructed on the edge of a large lake which now takes the same name.

In the 20th century areas were planted for forestry, predominately with conifers. In contrast to the more naturalistic earlier planting this forestry will gradually be replaced with broad-leaved native deciduous trees.

Top left: The Emperor Stream on East Moor

Bottom left: Emperor Lake

Top right: Stand Wood

Right: William Cowen; *Chatsworth from the foot of the Hunting Tower,* 1828

Opposite: Sam Henshaw doing a milking demonstration in the Farmyard

Above: Photograph of the Building Yard prior to conversion, 1972

Below: Peppa, a Large White Pig

FARMYARD AND ADVENTURE PLAYGROUND

People have always expressed an interest in learning about the land immediately surrounding Chatsworth, and Duchess Deborah was aware that teachers wanted their pupils to see working farms and forests. Her vision, therefore, was to create an educational exhibition, gathering a cross section of the farming and forestry activities at Chatsworth to explain how the land is used to produce food and other materials.

In 1972 the site of the farmyard and adventure playground was a derelict building yard. By 1973 the Farming and Forestry Exhibition opened on this site with a variety of animals. In the subsequent years the animal species increased to include dairy cows, beef cows, sheep, pigs, goats and poultry and with a milking parlour for demonstrations.

This working farmyard was developed as a representation of farming on the estate and British farming overall. The farmyard is proud to continue to work with this ethos and has an extensive and carefully planned breeding programme, including some breeds on the 'at risk' register, such as Berkshire and Tamworth pigs and Shire horses.

In 1983 the first playground was constructed next to Stand Wood with swings, slides, a fireman's pole and access via the 'secret tunnel'. A few years later the playground was redesigned as an adventure playground.

There is so much to see and do, with a full programme of events. There are courses on how to keep chickens and pigs, young farmhand days, craft activities, daily talks and demonstrations. From Easter to summer, and from Halloween to the popular nativity plays in the run up to Christmas when Bethlehem comes to the Oak Barn, the children take centre stage alongside many of the animals from the farmyard.

Today the farmyard and adventure playground continue to educate and entertain families and school groups on topical farming issues, regular demonstrations, animal handling and tractor trailer rides, with lots of interaction and fun, fulfilling the vision Duchess Deborah had over 40 years ago.

The stables were designed by James Paine (1717-1789) for the 4th Duke as part of the re-landscaping and naturalisation of the Park. The new 'Great Stables', as they are referred to in the building accounts, were prominently sited on rising ground behind the house. The foundations for the new building were laid in 1758, and the whole completed in 1766 with the installation of the coat-of-arms in the pediment, carved by Henry Watson, probably the grandson of Chatsworth's master carver Samuel Watson (1662-1715).

The stables are in the Palladian style of architecture, which had been championed by the 3rd Earl of Burlington, the 4th Duke's father-in-law. The building is approximately 60 metres (190 feet) square, making it larger in plan than the 1st Duke's house. The entrance to the stables on the west features a central clock tower, supported by massive Doric columns enriched with rusticated banding beneath the monumental coat-of-arms which incorporates real deer antlers on the carved stone stags.

The turret clock is signed by the clockmaker Joseph Kirk, who died in the 1740s. The structure and some elements of the clock are, however, much earlier and can be dated to the mid 16th century making it an extraordinary survival from Elizabethan Chatsworth. The layout of the mechanism is unique in clock horology.

Photograph of grooms with coach and horses in the Stables Courtyard, c.1900

The stables originally had stalls for 80 horses, including carriage horses, riding horses, hunters and cart horses. To care for the horses the building was fitted out with a blacksmith's shop and shoeing space, a washing box and two harness rooms. On the first floor there was accommodation for coachmen, outriders, strappers, grooms and stable boys. In addition the entire first floor on the south side was given over to the storage of grain. The horses were exercised under the covered ride which surrounds the courtyard, and the central fountain supplied fresh water direct from a spring in Stand Wood. In the 1830s the 6th Duke added a new Carriage House on the east side of the building to accommodate his and his guests' carriages.

In 1975 a small tea-bar was opened. This was quickly followed by a café in 1979. In 1991 the Carriage House was opened as a cafeteria restaurant. Today this restaurant provides 250 covers, and is complemented by the Cavendish Restaurant, which has waitress service dining and afternoon teas. There are further function spaces available for booked groups and since 2005 the stables has served as a venue for weddings. In addition there is a gift shop, a garden shop and a small area given over to produce from the larger off-site Chatsworth Estate Farm Shop.

Opposite: Dame Elisabeth Frink; Warhorse, 1992

Top: Photograph of horse and cart, 1920s

Bottom: The Garden Shop

Chatsworth has always had an excellent reputation for hospitality, and this tradition continues in the huge variety of original and welcoming accommodation across the estate and beyond.

From fine hotels and country inns with comfortable rooms and outstanding food, to self-catering homes from home, converted barns, cottages and the Elizabethan Hunting Tower, there is something for every taste.

There are three boutique hotels, where attention to detail runs through everything, from attractive decor and comfy beds to award winning food and thoughtful and attentive service.

THE CAVENDISH HOTEL, BASLOW

Chatsworth is easily reached from the Cavendish Hotel on foot or by car. This former coaching inn has an interesting collection of original paintings, prints and photographs, and a number of pieces of furniture from the stores at Chatsworth. From every bedroom there is a view of Chatsworth Park. Two AA Rosette food is available in a choice of two restaurants.

THE DEVONSHIRE ARMS, BEELEY

Set on the Chatsworth Estate, this award winning country inn with rooms boasts the character and charm of a historic inn with a contemporary twist. A modern Brasserie and a cosy bar, this inn has been completely refurbished by the Duchess.

THE DEVONSHIRE ARMS, PILSLEY

Two miles from Chatsworth and on the doorstep of the award winning Chatsworth Estate Farm Shop, this cosy inn serves local cask ales, freshly cooked food and has 13 bedrooms, all designed and decorated by the Duchess.

THE PERFECT HOME FROM HOME

Set in five locations on the Chatsworth Estate in Derbyshire and the Peak District, the Chatsworth Estate Holiday Cottages provide stylish, traditional comfort with contemporary design. The 12th Duke and Duchess take a great personal interest in the planning and decoration of the holiday cottages, and they are furnished with a mixture of old and new furniture, interesting pictures and good books.

The Chatsworth website details all the properties available for holiday rental for short or longer breaks. Chatsworth Estate Farm Shop produce can be ordered in advance and private chefs are available on request.

Situated on the Chatsworth Estate in close proximity to Chatsworth House, here are a few of the properties available, steeped in history and charm.

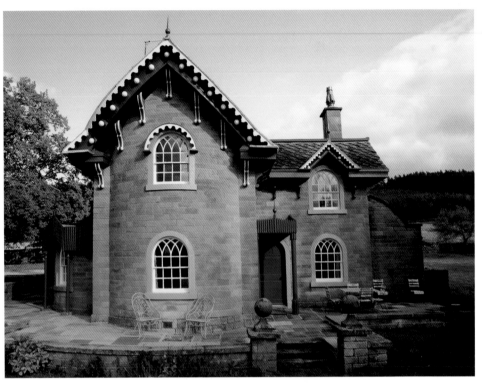

THE HUNTING TOWER

The tower stands on the escarpment 400 feet above Chatsworth House, on the edge of Stand Wood, with panoramic views of the Lancelot 'Capability' Brown landscape. Completed c.1582 for Bess of Hardwick, ancestress of the Dukes of Devonshire, to designs by the Elizabethan architect Robert Smythson.

SWISS COTTAGE

Swiss Cottage, overlooking its own lake, was built between 1839 and 1842 as part of the 6th Duke's many improvements to the Chatsworth Estate. It was designed as an 'eye-catcher' in the landscape, to be admired on carriage rides or walks around the estate. Two double and one twin bedrooms, all en-suite and a charming sitting room and kitchen provide a haven of peace, yet only 1½ miles from Chatsworth along a private road.

RUSSIAN COTTAGE

Russian Cottage was built after a gift of a model of a Russian Farm to the 6th Duke in 1855 from the brother of Tsar Nicholas of Russia. The Tsar and the 6th Duke had become friends following the 6th Duke's visit to Russia in 1816 when he served as the British Ambassador to Moscow. One double en-suite bedroom and one twin with bathroom across the hall.

GARDENER'S COTTAGE

A grade II listed building, built in the early 19th century, situated within Chatsworth Park. It was reported as the one house that remained in the historic village of Edensor, when the 4th Duke carried out his landscaping and park improvements. Two double and one twin bedrooms, all en-suite.

PARK COTTAGE

Park Cottage is a Grade II listed 17th century thatch cottage completely refurbished by the Duchess. One large double bedroom and a smaller single bedroom with a modern bathroom. A private path through woodland leads to the park and a 30 minute walk to Chatsworth.

Established by Duchess Deborah in 1977, the Chatsworth Estate Farm Shop sold beef and lamb from the estate farms, and venison from the park. Its aim was to sell Chatsworth's produce direct to people who wanted to eat the highest quality and locally grown food. Since then, the Estate Farm Shop has developed and diversified, going from strength to strength, to become an acknowledged leader in its field.

The Estate Farm Shop continues to be dedicated to protecting and nurturing the family-run working farm heritage. It aims to source primarily from the estate, secondly from tenant farms, thirdly from local food producers of Derbyshire and then from other quality suppliers within the UK wherever possible. Animal welfare is of the highest priority, and all farms are charged with breeding and rearing contented and healthy livestock. The Estate Farm Shop offers beef, lamb, poultry, free range pork and a wide selection of game from its butchery counter, freshly baked breads, cakes and biscuits from the bakery, a whole host of seasonal fruit and vegetables, as well as a wide range of pies, pastries, meats and cheeses from the delicatessen. The fresh fish counter provides a wide selection of daily catches, focusing especially on fish caught in British waters. The Estate Farm Shop Café was introduced in 1985 to offer seasonal, home cooked dishes in a warm and friendly environment. The café overlooks beautiful views of the park and estate.

Top: Duchess Deborah with butchers at the opening of the Estate Farm Shop, 1977

Bottom: Estate Farm Shop Café

After a thorough assessment in 2007 of the fabric of the building and its services, instigated by the 12th Duke and Duchess, a programme of essential repairs, maintenance and restoration was begun to preserve Chatsworth for the future. Some of the masonry is over 300 years old, and weathering and atmospheric pollution had caused it to deteriorate. Stone cleaning and exterior maintenance of the masonry continues, and parts of the house will be covered in scaffolding until 2017.

Inside, work continues to renew the essential services and improve the quality of insulation and Chatsworth's energy efficiency. All the plumbing and electrics are in the process of being replaced with safer and more effective technology. The visitor route has been increased with the creation of new galleries on the second floor of the main house and in the North Wing. The lift has been replaced and there is improved access to all rooms open to the visitors.

Beyond the house, other built structures are beginning to be conserved or restored including the Golden Gates, the Game Larder and Paine's Mill. The challenge of maintenance and improvement is huge. All income generated through visitor admission contributes to this ambitious programme of restoration and renewal. It is planned that in time resources will become available to address the preservation of the stables as part of this major capital investment.

Right: Vases above the balustrade over the south front in the process of stone cleaning, 2011

The collections of art and archives are also subject to a programme of ongoing conservation. Much work has already been done to safeguard these treasures for the future, but there is a substantial backlog of conservation still to be done. New displays in the house, and loans to exhibitions around the world have resulted in the conservation of many objects, from paintings and Old Master Drawings, to furniture, ceramics, textiles, sculpture and archives. In addition a rolling programme of conservation is undertaken each year, guided by an external panel of specialist advisors. The collections are managed by a multidisciplinary team of specialists whose work includes research and documentation, exhibition planning and delivery, as well as conservation and preservation. The collections are available for study by appointment.

Top right: The David Roentgen mahogany cylinder bureau undergoing conservation in the workshop of Arlington Conservation

Below: Detail of one of the armorial trophies from the Inner Court; before and after Restoration. 2009

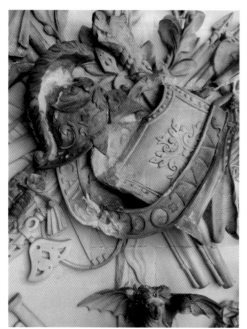

Top left: Restoration of the painted walls in the Painted Hall, 2006

Top right: Lynsay Shephard from Shephard Travis Textile Conservation Studio Ltd. washing a Mortlake tapestry

Left: Detail from the Mortlake Acts of the Apostles tapestries: The Healing of the Lame Man before and after washing

> *"Learning is at the heart of everything at Chatsworth."*
>
> Lord Burlington
> *Chairman, Devonshire Educational Trust*

The Devonshire Educational Trust was established in 2004, by the 12th Duke to provide educational opportunities and activities at Chatsworth and across the Devonshire estates, which are accessible and relevant for a broad range of people. The Trust undertakes a range of work at Chatsworth to promote and deliver educational activities focusing on the skills and assets; history, the arts and the environment.

The Trust supports learning for disadvantaged children and young people, and funds visits to Chatsworth for those who would not usually get the opportunity. With the support of the Chatsworth House Trust and other external funders including the Derbyshire Charity Clay Shoot, a range of educational projects have been completed in recent years. From outdoor educational activities and the conversion of the Stick Yard as an outdoor learning hub, to ARTiculation Discovery Days which seek to inspire and engage children in different types of art, helping them express their opinions and thoughts. Other recent projects include working in partnership with Derbyshire County Council through the Devonshire Project, to provide pre-school children in care and their carers, with a special day at the farmyard with lots of hands-on activities and farmyard fun.

Over the coming years the Devonshire Educational Trust is expanding its horizons, building on the good work thus far, with more opportunities for education and learning being developed at Chatsworth and across the Devonshire estate.

" We want to develop, steer and promote an evolving policy of environmental awareness and social responsibility, with a vision to ensure Chatsworth's on-going commitment to sustainability with the philosophy 'reduce, reuse, recycle' at its heart."

Lord Burlington
Chairman, Devonshire Group Environmental Committee

Lord Burlington, the son of the 12th Duke and Duchess, set up the Devonshire Group Environmental Committee to promote environmental awareness across the estate.

The Chatsworth hydro has been supplying electricity to the house since the 1890s and today new technologies continue to support the creation of renewable heat and power across the estate; a biomass boiler supplies heat to the estate office as well as several surrounding homes and most recently the Chatsworth Renewable Energy Centre opened adjacent to the kitchen garden. The centre houses a low carbon, combined heat and power gasification system, to feed the house, garden, stables shops and restaurants with 97% of electricity and 72% of heating demand.

Chatsworth looks for innovative ways to deal with waste, treating it as a valuable resource and not simply rubbish. The first ambition is to investigate if waste materials can be reused on site, if not it is segregated for recycling. If waste can't be reused or recycled it is sent to 'energy from waste facilities.' Landfill is a last resort.

To evolve the stewardship of the estates in the 21st century Chatsworth is now measuring three performance goals: first, social impact, second, environmental impact and third, economic impact (the way most organisations think about performance). Lord Burlington has coined them: People, Planet and Profit: together, Chatsworth's Triple Bottom Line.

Students from Alfreton Grange Arts College help open the Chatsworth Renewable Energy Centre with the Duke and Duchess. December 2013

Chatsworth has been handed down 16 generations of the Cavendish family. It is a family home, a working community and a living landscape. The house, many of its contents and 737 hectares (1822 acres) of the surrounding landscape are leased to a registered charity, the Chatsworth House Trust, established in 1981. The 12th Duke and Duchess pay rent to the charity to live at Chatsworth and work with the charity and others to welcome Chatsworth's visitors.

Every penny of visitor admission goes directly to the Chatsworth House Trust, which is dedicated to the long-term preservation of Chatsworth House, the art collection, garden, woodlands and park for the long term benefits of the public. The charity promotes the study and appreciation of Chatsworth as a place of historic, architectural and artistic interest and of natural beauty, and encourages the use and enjoyment of Chatsworth by visitors for education and recreation.

The charity continues to care for Chatsworth and a £14 million restoration project, known as the 'Masterplan', which began in 2008 is enabling visitors to experience the house, garden and estate as never seen before. This work and other essential projects can only happen thanks to the continuing support of visitors and the Friends of Chatsworth.

Above: Statue of Minerva on the apex of the pediment on the west façade of the house

Right: The Duchess being filmed for the BBC 1 documentary of Chatsworth, 2011 (with Sean Doxey, far right)

Chatsworth House Trust,
Bakewell, Derbyshire, DE45 1PP

Tel: 01246 565300, Email: visit@chatsworth.org

Text by Sally Ambrose, Matthew Hirst and Steve Porter

Photography by Paul Barker

Designed by Leap Design, Sheffield

Printed by Greenshires, Leicester

Project managed by Diane Naylor

Additional photography by:
Matthew Bullen: South Lawn 74, Concert in Garden
79, Statue of Flora 81, Coal Tunnel 91, Azaleas 94,
Pinetum 97, Bananas 103, Edensor, 106, Limousine
& Old Park 107, Stand Wood & Emperor Lake 111,
Nativity 114, Stables 117, Swiss Cottage 124

Simon Broadhead, Shoot Photography:
Duke and Duchess 5 & 18

David Dawson, Bridgeman Images: 55

Sylvain Deleu: North Sketch Sequence 56 & 57

Susan Jones: Country Fair 107;

Mark Kensett: Park 106, Hunting Tower & Swiss
Cottage 124

John Morley: Warhorse 118;

Diane Naylor: Burlington family 19, Deer 107,
Gardener's Cottage 123, Russian Cottage 125,
Masterplan 125 & 126,

National Trust Images: Bess of Hardwick 8

Gary Rogers: Camellia 82, Emperor Stream 111

Scene Photography: Canal Pond and South Front of
House 76 & 93

Nick Smith Photography: Hotels 123

David Vintiner: Old Master Drawing Cabinet 51,
Perfume Burner 48, Roentgen desk restoration 126

Claire Wood Photography Ltd: Milking 112

Archive and fine art photography from the
Devonshire Collection

ISBN 978-0-9537329-3-7

CAVENDISH FAMILY TREE

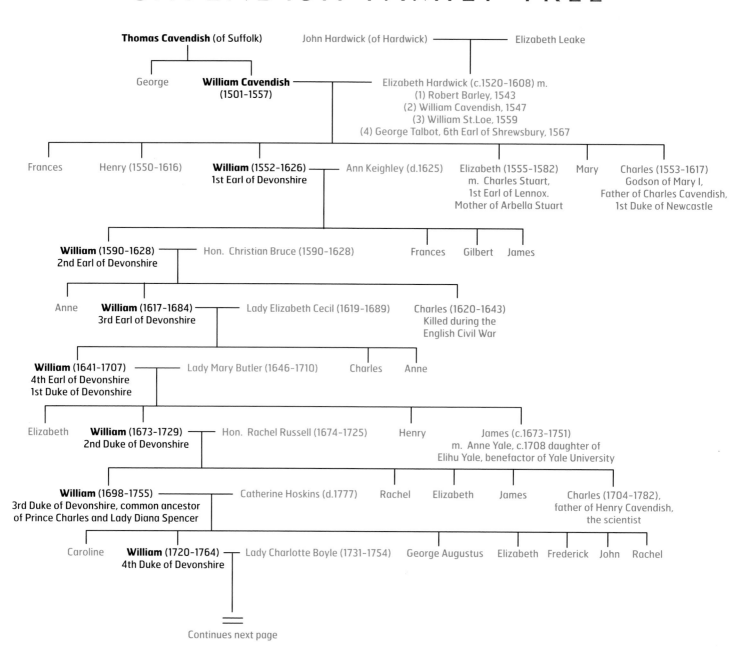

Thomas Cavendish (of Suffolk)

John Hardwick (of Hardwick) ——— Elizabeth Leake

George   **William Cavendish** (1501-1557)

Elizabeth Hardwick (c.1520-1608) m.
(1) Robert Barley, 1543
(2) William Cavendish, 1547
(3) William St.Loe, 1559
(4) George Talbot, 6th Earl of Shrewsbury, 1567

Frances   Henry (1550-1616)   **William (1552-1626)** 1st Earl of Devonshire ——— Ann Keighley (d.1625)   Elizabeth (1555-1582) m. Charles Stuart, 1st Earl of Lennox. Mother of Arbella Stuart   Mary   Charles (1553-1617) Godson of Mary I, Father of Charles Cavendish, 1st Duke of Newcastle

William (1590-1628) 2nd Earl of Devonshire ——— Hon. Christian Bruce (1590-1628)   Frances   Gilbert   James

Anne   **William (1617-1684)** 3rd Earl of Devonshire ——— Lady Elizabeth Cecil (1619-1689)   Charles (1620-1643) Killed during the English Civil War

William (1641-1707) 4th Earl of Devonshire 1st Duke of Devonshire ——— Lady Mary Butler (1646-1710)   Charles   Anne

Elizabeth   **William (1673-1729)** 2nd Duke of Devonshire ——— Hon. Rachel Russell (1674-1725)   Henry   James (c.1673-1751) m. Anne Yale, c.1708 daughter of Elihu Yale, benefactor of Yale University

William (1698-1755) 3rd Duke of Devonshire, common ancestor of Prince Charles and Lady Diana Spencer ——— Catherine Hoskins (d.1777)   Rachel   Elizabeth   James   Charles (1704-1782), father of Henry Cavendish, the scientist

Caroline   **William (1720-1764)** 4th Duke of Devonshire ——— Lady Charlotte Boyle (1731-1754)   George Augustus   Elizabeth   Frederick   John   Rachel

Continues next page

Continued from last page

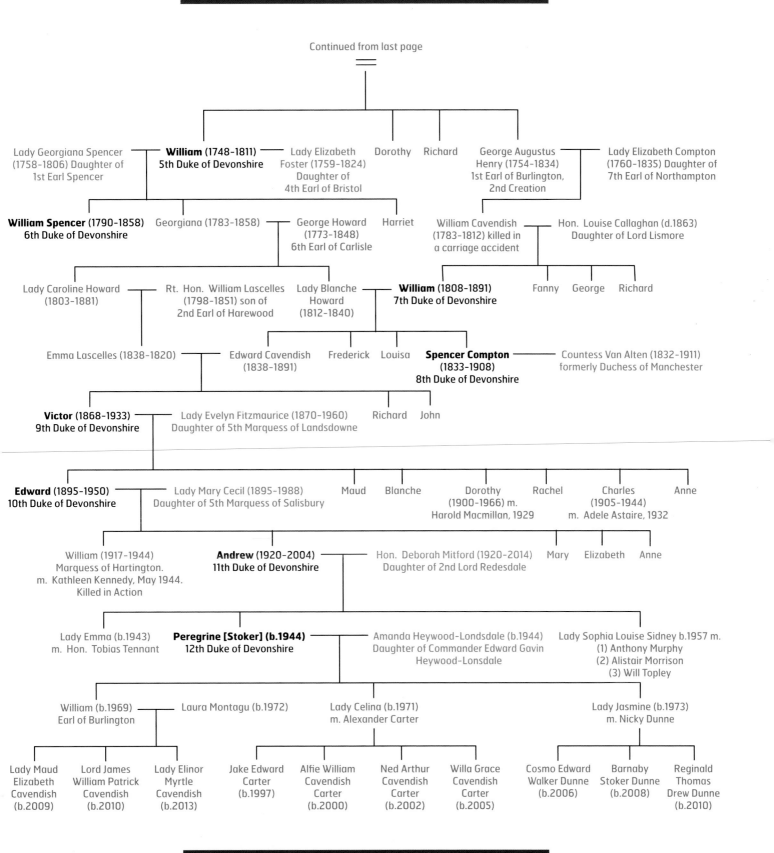

Lady Georgiana Spencer (1758-1806) Daughter of 1st Earl Spencer

William (1748-1811) 5th Duke of Devonshire

Lady Elizabeth Foster (1759-1824) Daughter of 4th Earl of Bristol

Dorothy

Richard

George Augustus Henry (1754-1834) 1st Earl of Burlington, 2nd Creation

Lady Elizabeth Compton (1760-1835) Daughter of 7th Earl of Northampton

William Spencer (1790-1858) 6th Duke of Devonshire

Georgiana (1783-1858)

George Howard (1773-1848) 6th Earl of Carlisle

Harriet

William Cavendish (1783-1812) killed in a carriage accident

Hon. Louise Callaghan (d.1863) Daughter of Lord Lismore

Lady Caroline Howard (1803-1881)

Rt. Hon. William Lascelles (1798-1851) son of 2nd Earl of Harewood

Lady Blanche Howard (1812-1840)

William (1808-1891) 7th Duke of Devonshire

Fanny   George   Richard

Emma Lascelles (1838-1820)

Edward Cavendish (1838-1891)

Frederick   Louisa

Spencer Compton (1833-1908) 8th Duke of Devonshire

Countess Van Alten (1832-1911) formerly Duchess of Manchester

Victor (1868-1933) 9th Duke of Devonshire

Lady Evelyn Fitzmaurice (1870-1960) Daughter of 5th Marquess of Landsdowne

Richard   John

Edward (1895-1950) 10th Duke of Devonshire

Lady Mary Cecil (1895-1988) Daughter of 5th Marquess of Salisbury

Maud   Blanche

Dorothy (1900-1966) m. Harold Macmillan, 1929

Rachel

Charles (1905-1944) m. Adele Astaire, 1932

Anne

William (1917-1944) Marquess of Hartington. m. Kathleen Kennedy, May 1944. Killed in Action

Andrew (1920-2004) 11th Duke of Devonshire

Hon. Deborah Mitford (1920-2014) Daughter of 2nd Lord Redesdale

Mary   Elizabeth   Anne

Lady Emma (b.1943) m. Hon. Tobias Tennant

Peregrine [Stoker] (b.1944) 12th Duke of Devonshire

Amanda Heywood-Londsdale (b.1944) Daughter of Commander Edward Gavin Heywood-Lonsdale

Lady Sophia Louise Sidney b.1957 m. (1) Anthony Murphy (2) Alistair Morrison (3) Will Topley

William (b.1969) Earl of Burlington

Laura Montagu (b.1972)

Lady Celina (b.1971) m. Alexander Carter

Lady Jasmine (b.1973) m. Nicky Dunne

Lady Maud Elizabeth Cavendish (b.2009)

Lord James William Patrick Cavendish (b.2010)

Lady Elinor Myrtle Cavendish (b.2013)

Jake Edward Carter (b.1997)

Alfie William Cavendish Carter (b.2000)

Ned Arthur Cavendish Carter (b.2002)

Willa Grace Cavendish Carter (b.2005)

Cosmo Edward Walker Dunne (b.2006)

Barnaby Stoker Dunne (b.2008)

Reginald Thomas Drew Dunne (b.2010)

Hunting
Tower

Stand
Wood

Old
Park

River Derwent

Edensor

B6012